The Lost Colonists
Their Fortune
and
Probable Fate

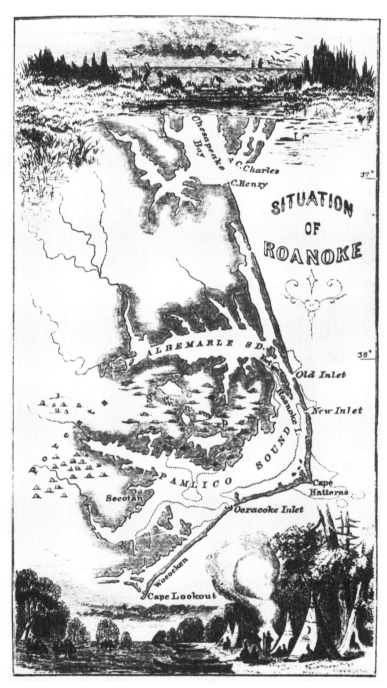

This largely hypothetical pictorial map of the northern coast of North Carolina was published ca. 1860. From Jacob Abbott, *American History* (New York: Sheldon and Company, 8 volumes, 1860–1865), III, 89.

The Lost Colonists

Their Fortune and Probable Fate

David Beers Quinn

Raleigh
America's Four Hundredth Anniversary Committee
North Carolina Department of Cultural Resources

NORTH CAROLINA DEPARTMENT OF CULTURAL RESOURCES
Linda A. Carlisle
Secretary

OFFICE OF ARCHIVES AND HISTORY
Jeffrey J. Crow
Deputy Secretary

DIVISION OF HISTORICAL RESOURCES
David L. S. Brook
Director

HISTORICAL PUBLICATIONS SECTION
Donna E. Kelly
Administrator

Cover—This fanciful engraving, made in the nineteenth century, represents John White at the time of his return to Roanoke Island in 1590. Reproduced from an early North Carolina textbook.

Printed by Edwards Brothers, Lillington, N.C.

Contents

Maps and Illustrations

Foreword

America's Four Hundredth Anniversary Committee, formed in 1978 under the provisions of an act of the North Carolina General Assembly of 1973, was charged with recommending plans for the observance of the quadricentennial of the first English attempts to explore and settle North America. The committee has proposed to carry out a variety of programs to appeal to a broad range of people. Among these is a publications program that includes a series of booklets dealing with the history of the events and people of the 1580s.

Queen Elizabeth I of England enjoyed a reign that was for the most part peaceful. It was a period of prosperity, which saw the flourishing of a new interest in literature, religion, exploration, and business. English mariners began to venture farther from home, and in time talk began to be heard of hopes to establish naval bases and colonies in America. Men of the County of Devon in the southwest of England, seafarers for generations, played leading roles in this expansion. One of these, Walter Ralegh (as he most often wrote his name), became a favorite of the queen, and on him she bestowed a variety of honors and rewards. It was he to whom she granted a charter in 1584 authorizing the discovery and occupation of lands not already held by "any Christian Prince and . . . people." Ralegh promptly sent a reconnaissance expedition to what is now North Carolina, and this was followed in due time by a colony under the leadership of Ralph Lane. Headquarters were established on Roanoke Island. After remaining for nearly a year and exploring far afield, Lane and his men returned to England in 1586.

In the summer of 1587 Gov. John White and a colony of 115 men, women, and children arrived and occupied the houses and the fort left by Lane. The brief annals of this colony are recorded in a journal kept by the governor; they tell of certain problems that arose early—but they also record the birth of the first English child in America. The journal further explains why Governor White consented to return to England for supplies. His departure was the last contact with the settlers who constituted the "Lost Colony," renowned in history, literature, and folklore.

Although a casual acquaintance with the facts of these English efforts might suggest that they were failures, such was far from the case. Ralegh's expenditures of time, effort, and resources (in which he was joined by many others, including Queen Elizabeth herself) had salutary effects for England and certainly for all of present-day America. From Ralegh's initial investment in the reconnaissance voyage, as well as from the colonies, came careful descriptions of the New World and samples of its products. The people of England, indeed of the Western world, learned about North America; because books were published based on what Ralegh's men discovered, they could soon read for themselves of the natives there and the promise of strange and wonderful new resources.

From these voyages and colonizing efforts came the conviction that an English nation could be established in America. In 1606, when another charter was about to be issued for further settlement, King James, who succeeded Queen Elizabeth at her death in 1603, called for advice from some of the men who had been associated with Ralegh. They assured the king that further efforts would surely succeed. With this the Virginia Company was chartered, and it established England's first permanent settlement in America at Jamestown.

Because of Sir Walter Ralegh's vision, England persisted. Because of England's persistence and its refusal to yield to Spain's claims to the region, the United States today enjoys an English heritage. English common law is the basis of American law; American legislative bodies are modeled on the House of Commons with the rights and freedoms that it developed over a long period of time; America's mother tongue is English, and it is the most commonly spoken language in the world—pilots and navigators on international airlines and the controllers who direct them at airports all over the world use English. Americans also share England's literary tradition: Chaucer, Beowulf, King Arthur, and Shakespeare are America's too, and Americans can enjoy Dickens and Tennyson, as well as Agatha Christie and Dorothy Sayers. America's religious freedom is also in the English tradition, and several of this nation's Protestant denominations trace their earliest history to origins in England; the Episcopal church, certainly, but the Quakers, Baptists, Congregationalists, and Universalists as well.

America's Four Hundredth Anniversary Committee has planned many programs to direct national and even international attention to the significance of events that occurred from bases established by English men, women, and children, but notably Sir Walter Ralegh, in what is now North Carolina during the period 1584–1590. While some of the programs may be regarded as fleeting and soon forgotten, the publications are intended to serve as lasting reminders of America's indebtedness to England. Books, pamphlets, and folders covering a broad range of topics have been prepared by authors on both sides of the Atlantic. These, it is anticipated, will introduce a vast new audience to the facts of America's origins.

Lindsay C. Warren Jr., *Chairman*
America's Four Hundredth Anniversary Committee

A Note on Ralegh

For the publications of America's Four Hundredth Anniversary Committee, it has been decided to use the spellings of certain surnames that were used by Elizabethan Englishmen themselves rather than modern versions of those names. Sir Walter Ralegh is not known to have used the spelling of his name that prevails today, although in his youth he did use a variety of other spellings. Every known signature of his from 1583 until his death in 1618 appears as *Ralegh*. The editors have also adopted the spelling of *Harriot* for Thomas Harriot (also spelled *Hariot*) and *Fernandes* for Simon Fernandes (also spelled *Fernandez* and *Ferdinando*), although variant spellings may also be found. For further information on Ralegh, see T. N. Brushfield, "Sir W. Ralegh: A Plea for a Surname," in *Report and Transactions of the Devonshire Association*, XVIII (1886), 450–461.

Acknowledgments

William S. Powell of the University of North Carolina at Chapel Hill has assisted in bringing this pamphlet to its final form. E. Randolph Turner, senior prehistoric archaeologist, Virginia Research Center for Archaeology, Yorktown; Helen C. Rountree, coordinator, Anthropology Curriculum, Department of Sociology and Criminal Justice, Old Dominion University, Norfolk, Virginia; Thomas C. Loftfield, Department of Sociology and Anthropology, University of North Carolina at Wilmington; and David S. Phelps, Department of Sociology and Anthropology, East Carolina University, Greenville, North Carolina, have provided most helpful information and opinions.

David Beers Quinn

Introduction

The Lost Colonists provide one of the first and most challenging mystery stories of American history. They may also present to us the first example of the assimilation of people from the British Isles with Native Americans, a result that did not take place to any great extent in eastern North America or, indeed, elsewhere in that great area. The writer on this subject has to be as accurate as he can, yet willing to speculate. There are clear factual accounts of the voyage of the colonists under the leadership of John White in 1587 and their temporary establishment on Roanoke Island. There is equally clear evidence that when John White returned to the island in 1590 the settlers had gone. All traces of their having lived there during the previous three years had disappeared. Only a newly built defensive fortification remained on the island. No person certainly belonging to the 1587 colony is known to have been seen again by a white man.

We have, however, clear evidence that white settlers identified as having come from Roanoke were living in the area between the Elizabeth River and what is now Cape Henry, in modern Virginia, during the twenty years after their presumed departure from Roanoke Island. We have equally positive evidence that colonists were killed by the Virginia Indian ruler Powhatan shortly before Jamestown was founded. But not all North Carolinians are prepared to accept this evidence because it is indirect and occurs a few years, perhaps only two or three years, after the event.

Intensive searches—but not intensive enough, we might think— were made for survivors of the colony in 1608, and seven persons were heard of as having escaped the killing and reached the Chowan tribe not far from the head of Albemarle Sound in North Carolina. Held incommunicado by the Indians there, they were lost sight of and finally forgotten by the Virginia settlers. It can be conjectured with a degree of probability that some of the colonists remained with the Europeanized Indian Manteo on the Carolina Outer Banks near modern Cape Hatteras. All trace of these people was lost, however, and their subsequent fate is totally unknown, though speculation has suggested that they formed an element in later Indian populations on the Carolina sounds.

In assimilating the materials that survive on the Lost Colonists and their fate, there are many gaps in our documentation. These must be filled by working conjectures. Historians, especially of earlier periods of history, have to make assumptions that blend the materials at their disposal into a coherent story while carefully admitting where they are and are not relying directly on documents (which may be good or only imperfect evidence). Otherwise they could not make any sense of their reconstruction of an often poorly documented past. In what follows, assumptions have been made and conjectures proposed that are the best that one historian can do with the materials at his disposal. They do not lead to any dramatic conclusion except that the great majority of the Lost Colonists, after nearly twenty years of life alongside or mingled with the Indians living to the south of Chesapeake Bay, across the border from North Carolina in modern Virginia, were wiped out in a massacre by the despotic ruler of the Indian tribes of tidewater Virginia. But our knowledge leads thereafter to strong indications, if not proof, that seven survivors remained in the possession (as slaves?) of a chief who dominated the Chowan River and possibly the lower reaches of the Roanoke River valley around 1608. There is also a probability that the younger men left on Roanoke Island in 1587 did not rejoin the main body of settlers but lived instead with the Croatoan (Hatteras) Indians of the Outer Banks.

There are bound to be differences of opinion as to what weight should be given each item of direct and indirect evidence. If new solutions are to be found, they must rest either on new documents (the finding of which is unlikely, if not impossible) or, most probably, on archaeological discoveries. If the Lost Colonists lived some twenty years on a site that, it is suggested, was well inland near the present Elizabeth River in Virginia, they are bound to have left traces that Powhatan is unlikely to have destroyed completely. Such a discovery would be thrilling for all North Carolinians and Virginians, but there is no assurance that it will ever take place. Nevertheless, it is our best hope of solving what appears to be the crucial element in the mystery of the Lost Colonists and their fate.

I. The Setting

A poignant and evocative picture stands at the beginning of the history of white settlement in North Carolina, England's first Virginia. It is one of eighty-nine men, seventeen women, and eleven children, two of them born on North American soil, left on Roanoke Island on August 27, 1587, and never seen again by European eyes. This mental picture, true or distorted, has remained in the modern North Carolina consciousness as a beginning that might have been—a procession of men, women, and children into a wilderness from which there was no return. It must haunt any celebration of the beginnings of English settlement in North Carolina and in North America as a whole in the sixtieth decade after the event.

And yet we know that North America was not a wilderness but that it had been occupied for some thousands of years by a gradually evolving Native American population, misnamed by Columbus and Pope Alexander VI as Indians. These people had cleared the understory for hunting through the woods, marked out trails for their travels from one village to another, plotted notional hunting grounds for communities ranging in size from small bands to major tribal entities, and maintained temporary seashore campsites at which the gathering of seafood was based. They had built villages, some of which were movable on short notice, that were genuine centers of communities, with religious ceremonial sites either inside or outside their limits and with small, carefully tilled and planted fields of corn, beans, squashes, sunflowers, maypops, and tobacco. The villages were served by dugout canoes of considerable strength and capacity, and those on the coast were supplied by elaborate fishweirs from which part of their sustenance was derived. Oysters especially, but crabs and other crustacea as well, formed a major part of the Indians' diet. Agriculture, hunting, and fishing were supplemented by the gathering of wild fruits (particularly nuts and berries) and the digging of roots, some of which were used for medicinal and ceremonial purposes. There was a social hierarchy of captured slaves (sometimes), common people, elders whose conciliar influence was considerable, and a ruling family from which successive chiefs were drawn, usually by matrilinear succession. These chiefs had power, but not unlimited power. They might by tradition, personality, or success in war dominate more than one community or even a substantial number of settlements; their power could extend outward in circles of diminishing influence.

Indian tribal groups were not isolated. The Indians were traders, making contact with others with whom advantageous exchanges could be made. The men were fighters whose bows and arrows, spears, and clubs were formidable weapons and who had well-developed techniques of both irregular and formal warfare, resorted to for reasons of economic or territorial expansion. Inside the communities there was division of labor. Men did the basic work of site clearing and tree burning, built the pole framework for houses, carved and burned out tree trunks for boats, took a major part in seafood gathering, and devoted much of their time to hunting deer (the basic protein in their diet), bears, and other animals, as well as edible birds. Women cultivated the gardens and small fields, prepared skins, beads, and dyes, made the pottery used for cooking maize and other vegetable and animal products (fish and venison particularly), and put by reserves of dried fish and corn for winter use or for seed corn. They probably also made nets, and they certainly produced reed mats and woven baskets. They made and decorated the simple skin clothing worn by both sexes. There were priests to conduct ceremonies relating to the dead, whose spirits were thought to influence the lives of the living; there was the shaman or medicine man who could conduct ceremonies for the placation of spirits, foretell the future, and mend the hurts of the sick or wounded—probably with as much or more success than European doctors of the time. Above all, the Indians were numerous and had a strong attachment to their land.

In considering the Lost Colonists realistically, therefore, any idea that these English people in 1587 were alone must be abandoned. They were intruders surrounded by a population that scholars now consider much denser than was formerly thought. The Native Americans were often kind and helpful to the strangers, since they could learn from them different customs and habits and new techniques of living. The Indians could exchange their own food and products for novel European goods; metal was especially desirable. There was land to spare—cleared sites that had been abandoned because fertility had declined but that were recovering—where the inhabitants might tolerate the presence of a strange community. At first the Indians felt that the Europeans came from another world, but soon they came to realize that the newcomers were human like themselves.

In spite of the powerful guns and swords of the Europeans, the Indians were not afraid to challenge the continuance of their colonies when this seemed desirable or necessary. Although the numbers of settlers arriving between 1584 and 1587 were too small to be a lasting danger to the native way of life, the Indians of later Virginia would rebel forcibly when substantial parts of their lands were taken away. There were not xenophobic, however, and a small community such as that of the 1587 settlers—the Lost Colonists—had little to fear unless its attitudes and actions were hostile or unless the relative wealth of its possessions, especially in metals, aroused Native American cupidity. The chances that a group of something over 100 persons, including women and children, would be well treated were good. The Lost Colonists disappeared, therefore, into a land already inhabited and developed, where they might assimilate or remain separate. Their fate and fortune lay in the hands of the native people.

II. The Colonists Land
on Roanoke Island

The colony that Gov. John White led from England to Roanoke Island between April and late July 1587 represented the second undertaking of Sir Walter Ralegh, the royal grantee of as much North American soil as he could occupy. Ralegh, who held his authority as lord and governor of Virginia from Queen Elizabeth I, had learned from Philip Amadas and Arthur Barlowe, commanders in the reconnaissance in 1584 (as well as from the Indians Manteo and Wanchese, who had come with them from America to England), something of the attractions of the Carolina sounds and banks. In 1585 he had sent a colony under Sir Richard Grenville to establish a foothold there. This was partly a garrison and established an English presence on territory that the Spanish in Florida and the Caribbean regarded as their own. But the colonists were also to explore, examine the human, natural, and physical resources of the region, and report on its possibilities. This they did between July 1585 and June 1586, after which they unexpectedly arrived back in England with Sir Francis Drake toward the end of July. Much of what they said was good. The region was attractively covered with vegetation and, where cleared, was fertile (though the clearings were the work of the Indians, not of nature), while it was also healthy, with winters not as cold as in England. But Roanoke Island had limited resources, and the whole area lacked any great agricultural or mineral attractions, though rumors of copper and possibly gold in the distant interior circulated. However, there was no good harbor along the Outer Banks, and devastating storms could destroy shipping anchoring off the shores.

One of the exploring parties had lived for part of the winter farther north, in the area south of Chesapeake Bay, and had found the region more open and fertile and the Indians friendly. Their camp lay probably in an Indian village some considerable way up the modern Elizabeth River to the south of present-day Norfolk. This group learned that they were close to an inland sea, Chesapeake Bay, and they were able, as they explored, to see the southern shore, the mouth of the James River, and even the southern tip of the modern Virginia Eastern Shore.

The colony's governor, Ralph Lane, had heard independently of the depth and extent of Chesapeake Bay from the Chowanoac chieftain Menatonon and had been anxious to explore there. But a storm in June, which also disrupted Drake's fleet at anchor near the Outer Banks, checked plans to reconnoiter the bay from the ocean side.

Nonetheless, the 1587 colony was chosen and equipped to act as a new kind of settlement—a small, largely self-supporting community that would live close to the south shore of Chesapeake Bay with or alongside the Chesapeake Indians, who had aided the English visitors in 1585–1586 and who would, it was expected, help and protect the new settlers until they became established. Then, perhaps, the bay itself might become the base for English shipping that the Outer Banks so conspicuously had failed to be, though no decision had been made on this vital point when the colony left England. Nor could it be foreseen how relations with the native peoples of the region might be affected if the English settlement developed into a major occupation of the land and a base for shipping to operate against the Spanish.

Little is known of the social composition of the 1587 colony. Prof. William S. Powell's preliminary attempts at identification of the colonists, though incomplete and often inconclusive, have provided some basic information that it is hoped he will expand. However, the difficulty of identifying ordinary people and the question of whether or not the use of names alone is an accurate guide make the pursuit of this subject very difficult. It is known that an appreciable number of the individuals were London citizens and were probably mostly craftsmen from the lesser City of London companies, while others were most likely agricultural smallholders or even yeomen from the counties near the Thames and from Hampshire and perhaps Devon and Cornwall. A few had Welsh names; two Irishmen deserted on the way, but there may have been one or two left. There were possibly also one or two educated men among them who had attended one or other of the universities and were willing to take their chances in the New World. At least some of the colonists may have been puritans in the broader sense; that is, they lamented that the Church of England was not Protestant enough and was becoming too greatly dominated by bishops, and they sought purer forms of worship, though without any desire to separate from the Anglican community as a whole. It is clear that the colonists were all people from the middle or lower social strata, intending to work for their livings at agriculture or specialized crafts and to form the nucleus of an English society on American soil.

The presence of at least two pregnant women among the settlers when they left Portsmouth on April 26, 1587, shows a strong impetus to seek a new life away from plague-ridden London and the depressed agriculture of the time. There were offers of land—500 acres for each adventurer in person was a great fortune—to speed them on. Sir Walter Ralegh did not finance the colony directly. John White, the leader and governor, had an ambition, resulting from his year in the 1585–1586 colony, to plant an English community in America. He himself was a member of one of the smaller craft companies of the City of London, the Painter-Stainers, and it was probably among his like that he discovered considerable support for the new enterprise. He found Ralegh willing to incorporate the adventurers into a company to which lands in the Chesapeake area could be assigned *en bloc* and largely unseen (with no consideration of Native American rights).

To give the colonists status, their settlement on Chesapeake Bay was to be called from the first a city, "the Cittie of Ralegh in Virginia." Moreover, the governor and twelve assistants were made gentlemen, as none of them had held this rank. They were awarded grants of arms for their city and for themselves individually, and no doubt a ceremony took place when these were conferred. Perhaps it coincided with the marriage of White's daughter, Elenor, to one of the assistants, Ananias Dare. Three of the twelve assistants were to remain in London to ensure continued contact and supplies, while the other nine were to accompany the governor, John White, to Virginia.

It was expected that 150 persons would be ready to sail in the spring of 1587, but to collect enough money and stores in time may well have been difficult. We believe that Ralegh assumed responsibility for the cost of their transportation, though without direct evidence on this point. Selling their property, assembling their goods and chattels, and last-minute changes of mind—some men must have decided not to risk their wives and children in the attempt—hampered the preparations of many prospective colonists, so that only 118 persons planning to stay (or perhaps one or two fewer) finally set sail. One of the assistants, who decided at some point that he did not intend to remain, was the chief pilot, Simon Fernandes (Simão Fernandes originally), a Portuguese Protestant who had led the 1584 expedition of Amadas and Barlowe to an inlet in the banks near Roanoke Island but whose personal character was, to say the least, dubious. He had been a pirate and had behaved badly on an English expedition in the South Atlantic in 1582–1583.

The voyage out was unhappy, since White and Fernandes constantly quarreled. It may well be that Fernandes wished to attack and steal from Spanish ships in the Caribbean and that, when White resisted him to avoid hazarding the lives of his vulnerable company by warlike activities, the pilot interfered with his commander's plans. Two Irishmen slipped away to the Spaniards, but the rest of the expedition arrived safely at Hatarask Inlet, somewhat to the north of modern Oregon Inlet, on July 22 (by modern dating, August 1). When White prepared to go ashore to consult with fifteen or eighteen men left there by Sir Richard Grenville in 1586 (they were sent to reinforce Lane's colony but arrived too late), Fernandes delivered his final blow. He deposited the whole body of settlers on the island and the ships did not go on, as planned, to Chesapeake Bay.

The arrival of the English at Roanoke Island is depicted in this fanciful engraving, which was probably produced in the nineteenth century. From a copy owned by William S. Powell.

This disruption of their plans was at least a minor disaster to the colonists, since it was already late in the year for establishing a new settlement. Food stores and supplies would have to last them until the following summer, and they could not grow corn for themselves but would have to depend on Indian surpluses, if available. And the local Indians, formerly inhabiting Roanoke Island but at this time residing on the adjacent mainland, had become hostile to Ralph Lane, who had their chieftain, Wingina, killed in June 1586. Later in the year, they had killed several of Sir Richard Grenville's men and driven the others away.

The colonists were glad to reach land, however, even though White, James Lasie, and probably John Wright were the only persons among them who had been there before. Structures from the previous settlement survived to receive them. The fort perimeter was eroded, but the command post may have been largely intact (though White's statement on this is ambiguous) and the 1585 cottages were still reparable. After the initial unlading there was a quick rehabilitation of the old buildings but no attempt to raise new fortifications. Two friendly Indians, Manteo and Towaye, accompanied the settlers and gave advice. This was Manteo's second return to his homeland. He had gone to England in 1584 and returned in 1585, and he was taken back to England for another nine months in 1586–1587. Manteo was the colonists' most important sponsor and adviser in the new land. About Towaye nothing is known; he may have been Manteo's servant.

Manteo's community was located on Croatoan Island, his mother being the head of the band or tribe living there. The Outer Banks were then wide and wooded and supported some cultivation and settlement in villages bordering Pamlico Sound, at least near present-day Buxton and farther south on what is now Hatteras Island. We know that some of these shoreside settlements were small and were unlikely to have supported a substantial population of either Indians or Europeans.

In his narrative White tells us more about the ceremonies of the next few weeks than about how the settlers established themselves in their temporary homes. The entrusting of Roanoke Island and the surrounding area to Manteo as Queen Elizabeth's trustee illustrated the transitional nature of the English settlement. Manteo's baptism and installation took place alongside the joyful christening of the first child born on the island, Virginia Dare, John White's granddaughter (though there was to be another birth very soon). These are the points that catch the eye of the historian and are the highlights of what is known of the Lost Colony. But more serious matters had to be considered, the most important being the planned transfer of the colonists fifty miles northward into the interior.

White could give descriptions and maps of the route to be followed to the north, of Indian villages, and of the outline of the southern part of the Chesapeake Bay so far as he knew it; he could probably also provide details of personalities in the Chesapeake tribe. These Indians

This representation of the 1587 baptism of the Indian Manteo was painted by William Steene ca. 1930. A similar painting by the same artist shows the baptism of Virginia Dare, the first child of English parents to be born in the New World. Photograph from copy in the North Carolina Collection, Wilson Library, University of North Carolina at Chapel Hill.

would, he seems to have thought, welcome the permanent visitors. Perhaps messengers were even sent north to tell them to expect the settlers. Some of the colonists must surely have been taught something of the native language by Thomas Harriot before they left England, and White, who knew some himself, may have continued the instruction on the way out. Lasie and Wright may also have had some competence in the language, and Manteo and Towaye might have helped. The English were thus in some ways equipped to deal with the unexpected situation. Yet, it presented great perils for men and women so inexperienced in American conditions.

After hearing the reports brought back in 1586, the Reverend Richard Hakluyt, who had been Sir Walter Ralegh's adviser since he began his colonizing ventures, wrote from Paris, where he was chaplain and secretary to the ambassador, and advised Ralegh firmly that "your best planting will be about the bay of the 'Chesepians.'" Barlowe in 1584 had heard of Skicóac, a Chesapeake town known as a great settlement, a veritable city, from the Roanoke Indians: "Six days further [from Roanoke Island] is situate their greatest city, called 'Schycoake,' which this people affirm to be very great, but the savages were never at it, only they speak of it by the report of their fathers and other men, whom they have heard affirm it to be above one day's journey about." An Indian settlement with a circuit of approximately twenty miles was never seen or heard of in eastern North America in aboriginal times. Mythical though it was, this vague but exciting report no doubt influenced Ralph Lane in 1585 to send a party including John White and Thomas Harriot north to visit the place under "the colonel of the Chesepians," as Lane called him (though it is not known who he was).

Ralph Lane's account of the experiences of this party, which stayed in the area late in 1585 and early in 1586, was brief but informative:

The territory and soil of the "Chesepians" (being distant fifteen miles from the shore) was for pleasantness of seat, for temperature of climate, for fertilitie of soil, and for the commodity of the sea, besides multitude of bears (being an excellent good victual, with great woods of sassafras and walnut trees) is not to be exceeded by any other whatsoever.

Here, it might seem, Lane is clearly thinking of Skicóac rather than the area around Lynnhaven Bay, and this would be well inland along the Elizabeth River. His phrase "pleasantness of seat" implies that it would be an attractive place to live. His commendation of the fertility of the soil indicates a contrast with the type of soil on Roanoke Island. The very limited area of good-quality ground there constituted an important reason why a colony such as White's could not establish itself permanently on the island.

White's emphasis on the accessibility of seafood was borne out by what could then be found not only in the Elizabeth River but also on the shores of Chesapeake Bay itself, not many miles distant. The Great Dismal Swamp would be noted for its bears for centuries, and we can imagine White and Harriot, with their companions, shooting bears during the time they spent near the northern edge of the swamp. The animals might indeed have been good food, but their presence in considerable numbers could have proved something of a deterrent to people from the cities, towns, and countryside of southern England, where there was no such large and potentially dangerous beasts. Black walnut and hickory trees grew extensively around new and old Indian sites, as the Indians used the nuts for their oil as well as for their food value. Sassafras (the root, the bark, and even the wood) was sought for its supposed medicinal qualities, the pleasant-smelling emollient liquid derived from the roots, bark, and leaves in particular being credited with the capacity to cure many diseases, even syphilis. At the time Lane wrote, sassafras was a very valuable commodity and would give colonists in the area at least one salable product for export.

This is all that has come down to us as background information concerning the colonists' knowledge of the Chesapeake area. It is not much, but we can be sure that both Harriot and White left full written and pictorial records of this area that have not survived and that John White had a store of knowledge of its advantages and disadvantages that he conveyed to the more responsible men and women among the colonists. The territory for which they were bound was thus not wholly foreign to English experience, and they were going to a place that had already been reconnoitered for the purpose of settlement. This was calculated to help them to a considerable degree in overcoming the initial pains and trials of settlement, in spite of the trouble that Simon Fernandes had inflicted on them by leaving them on Roanoke Island instead of within easy reach of their new home, the planned "Cittie of Ralegh," and forcing on them a further journey over water and land.

III. The Colonists Stay on the Island When John White Goes for Help

The unloading of stores from the broad-bottomed flyboat occupied much of the colonists' time, since these had to be taken through Roanoke Sound in ships' boats and the pinnace. The latter, with no doubt a boat or two, was to be left with the settlers. The removal of cannon, bars of iron, and other heavy equipment from Roanoke Island to Chesapeake Bay must have given much concern to the settlers, but they probably thought the pinnace was adequate to do this. What became obvious was that if they had to rely to a great extent on their own resources until the following summer, then the stores they had were pitifully inadequate. Someone, it was felt, must ensure that new supplies were brought as soon as possible. In the original plan these would have been sent directly to Chesapeake Bay, but in the existing situation it is likely that they would be directed first to Roanoke Island, so that indications could be found there about the precise location to which they should be transported. But how could the supply vessels get effective directions? It was decided, after much heart-searching and after delivering a clearance to him for his action, that White himself must go to England to ensure that stores would be sent. Apparently it was agreed that a party of colonists would stay at Roanoke Island with the pinnace to await the return of the supply ships and then guide them to the new settlement. At the very least, White would have been assured that there would be *someone* on Roanoke Island to lead him to the exact place of settlement when he returned. The assumption that something like this was planned must lie behind any rational explanation of what followed.

How would this party be selected, and how numerous must it be? These questions cannot be answered precisely, but obviously it had to be a party stronger than that of the fifteen or eighteen men that Grenville left to be driven away in 1586 (though Manteo could have stood guard with his own men to aid in some degree). The group likely consisted of some twenty-five men, old and young, probably all unmarried. This would have left the colonists destined for their new settlement on Chesapeake Bay reduced in number to some sixty men, together with the twenty-seven women and children—fewer than 100 altogether. White tells us that they were getting ready for a journey of some fifty miles at the time he left the island and, from existing evidence, this could only be to the site originally designated for the colony on Chesapeake Bay. These people were to be the courageous ones, going into what they considered a wilderness to make a new home on American soil.

But the hardship for White was no less severe. He had to leave his family, his colonists, and the fate of the whole enterprise in other hands. His miserable experience on the way home in the flyboat, beset by accident and weather, and his landfall in Ireland, not England, must have left him disheartened as he arrived at last at Southampton on November 8, something over six months after he had set out from nearby Portsmouth. The story of his failure to return to Roanoke Island as he had so solemnly promised is sad and well known.

Ralegh and Grenville determined to establish a fortified post on Chesapeake Bay to act against Spain. Providing a squadron sufficiently strong to menace the treasure fleets that were Spain's lifeline had become a realistic way of diverting Spanish attention from the "Enterprise of England" (the overthrow of Queen Elizabeth I). But because the Great Armada was at this time known to be almost ready to sail, threatening England's continued existence, the American diversion was put to one side. The squadron was accordingly forbidden to sail and was sent to join Drake's fleet at Plymouth, where every ship with any capacity for warfare was sorely needed. White was not able to sail before the departure of the main squadron, since in winter exit from the English Channel, especially for small vessels, was often impossible for months at a time.

Finally, on April 5 by English reckoning and April 15 by ours, White slipped away with two small pinnaces bearing only fifteen additional planters and some stores but showing that there was still life in the venture, even though no more aid could be quickly mobilized. Yet this was encouraging to White, since by quick sailing direct to the Outer Banks, as Grenville had managed in 1586, he should arrive there by early July or even late June (though he had originally hoped to get there by Easter). The sad story of how the travelers got almost to the Azores, nearly halfway across the ocean, and were battered, robbed, and wounded by pirates, then worked their way back to England scarcely alive, is a tragedy few connected with the venture could bear to dwell on.

The best Ralegh could or would do, with his heavy official duties during and after the Armada campaign, was to try to arrange some administrative and financial backing for the colonists in the City of London. The backers he assembled in early March 1589, though they included wealthy and active merchants as well as the planner and historian Richard Hakluyt, somehow did not succeed in getting White back on his way in 1589. This is strange, and it has not been possible to explain it. Although there was still an embargo on foreign voyages, some exceptions were made to the ban; and it is curious that White did not qualify for one, as well as for the release of at least one substantial ship and a pinnace to enable him to make a safe passage. His credit, and even that of Ralegh, in the City of London was evidently poor, since enough money spent in the right places could have brought exemptions from the prohibitions, especially as the lord high admiral, Lord Howard of Effingham, had contributed to the earlier expedition in 1585.

The fretting, fearful year White passed we can scarcely imagine. By 1590 when William Sanderson, one of the merchant backers, was preparing his ship *Moonlight* to take stores to the colony, the delay was too great for White to bear. Finally Ralegh, at White's insistence, secured him passage on a privateer, the *Hopewell*, which (with its two consorts) was bound for a rendezvous with the *Moonlight* at a chosen point off the coast of Hispaniola; the meeting duly took place. But the voyage and the successful privateering campaign in the Caribbean meant that it took from March 20 to August 15 for the *Hopewell* and the *Moonlight* to reach Hatarask, so that just under three years had passed, instead of the six to eight months that White had hoped for, since the colonists had been left on Roanoke Island.

IV. The Colony Divides

What happened to the colonists in the years 1587 to 1590 is almost entirely a matter for conjecture. It may be that evidence will emerge in due course from archaeological searches, but the most we can do now is use our historical imagination, aided by what is known to be possible, to make up a tentative picture of the sequence of events. In the first place, there would have been a fairly rapid departure by the majority group of colonists. If they were to settle, as White said they planned to do when he left them, "50 miles into the maine," namely, not far from the southern shore of Chesapeake Bay where he and Harriot had been over the winter of 1585–1586, they would have to hurry to establish themselves before winter. It may be suggested that they sent a colonist who knew a little of the local Algonquian language, together with an Indian guide, as a messenger to the Chesapeake Indians to tell them they were on their way. The settlers would pack all the possessions they could carry and set out within a few weeks after White left. They would use the pinnace and some boats and canoes to carry them to the head of Currituck Sound and Back Bay, which probably extended farther north then, as early maps suggest, or else up the North Landing River, so that boats and canoes could take them a fair distance on their way. But sooner or later they had to go ashore and carry their possessions westward, most likely toward Skicóac. They possibly had the assistance of a small number of Manteo's tribe, but more probably did not, since evidence of any continuing contact between the Chesapeake Indians and those of the Carolina sounds has not been established. If the North Landing River was viable for canoes as far as the present-day North Landing, it was (swamps permitting) only a few miles overland to the vicinity of Great Bridge on the southern branch of the Elizabeth River. An alternative solution is that the pinnace was able to make two or three journeys around Cape Henry to, or almost to, the colony's destination.

Where did the group go? Is the vicinity of Skicóac the most likely area? Our best assumption is that their destination was where White, Harriot, and their party had remained in the winter of 1585–1586 and thus the location that Lane had briefly described as most suitable for settlement. James Lasie and John Wright (if they were with these colonists) might have been able to guide them to the place. As has been said, White had no doubt furnished all possible directions when he left. On the White-Harriot map Skicóac, on the southern branch of what was to be called the Elizabeth River and some twelve to fifteen miles due south of modern Hampton Roads, was prominently marked. Certainly, they could have had protection near there from the Powhatan Indians of the James and York rivers, known to be hostile to Europeans, since the Chesapeake Indians were quite separate from the growing realm under the leader Powhatan's dominance. In making this supposition it is necessary to assume that Skicóac was not on the edge of the Great Dismal Swamp, though it could not have been too far from it.

At Skicóac there probably would have been clearings in the nearby forest where Indian villages had formerly stood and where only relatively low second-growth forest would need to be removed before shelters could be built and land prepared for spring sowing. Alternatively, parts of this area may have been virtually unforested, making the choice of a location much easier. On such a site we can reasonably suppose that the eighty to 100 men, women, and children erected pole-and-frame shelters and collected fuel from the woods for cooking and heating. They lived on the provisions they had brought with them (these could not have been many) and on what the Indians could spare in the way of corn and dried fish, as well as fresh seafood that they caught before the end of the season. They probably killed deer, bears, and other animals for meat. If this assumption is acceptable thus far, it can further be supposed that the Chesapeake Indians proved friendly and cooperative, both because they remembered their pleasant dealings with the Englishmen on their earlier visit and because the English brought women and children with them, indicating their peaceful intentions.

It is again necessary to assume that in the spring of 1588 the colonists planted gardens of English seed as well as corn, beans, and possibly tobacco, perhaps obtained from the Indians. Learning the Indian ways of fishing and hunting would have kept them from going hungry. Increasingly, though, they would lack European amenities such as cooking utensils, iron and metal objects of all sorts, and clothes that could not be supplied from skins. Yet, in the first year they would be buoyed up by the expectation that White would appear, either overland with the party left on the island, or with their pinnace, or by sailing directly into the bay with a new fleet. They would be wholly disappointed in 1588.

In making these conjectures, the locations of two village sites on White's map—Chesepiuc, apparently on Great Neck in Lynnhaven Bay, and Apasus (added in the engraved version of the map published in 1590), near the western end of Lynnhaven Bay—can very tentatively be eliminated. There may have been open ground inland from these villages, and recent archaeological investigations have identified two Indian sites in this general area. What remained of one has been excavated, but no European artifacts have yet been found. However, the colonists would certainly have been less secure there from any Powhatan Indian interference than if they were located inland on the Elizabeth River.

On the other hand, what can be visualized about the men left on Roanoke Island? The old framed houses, evacuated and with all movable objects taken from them by the main body of colonists, would be of little value except as firewood. The command building, if it had survived inside the virtually useless fort perimeter, is unlikely to have been rehabilitated to any great degree, though it may well have served them temporarily. The main preoccupation of this small group was security. There were still remnants of the former Indian inhabitants of the island in the area, and they had shown their continued hostility by the killing of George Howe, one of the assistants, soon after the colonists first landed. It may have been around the site of the houses built in 1585 and temporarily restored in 1587 (not the site of the fort entrenchments of 1585–1586 and the command building of 1585–1587) that they built an enclosure—the place described by White in 1590 as "very strongly enclosed with a high palisado of great trees, with curtains and flankers very Fort-like" and with a main entrance about which he did not give details. Construction of the palisade involved considerable labor, and it must have taken some time to complete. What else the men remaining on Roanoke did—hunting, fishing, trading for corn up Albemarle Sound, or the like—can only be guessed. It cannot even be established that they stayed on the island for any considerable time.

Manteo is likely to have helped them from the beginning, though, and it is probable that they assisted him in his return, conveying him in the pinnace to his home on Croatoan, his mother's village in the vicinity of modern Cape Hatteras (in the woods to the southwest of Buxton) and a day's sail south of Roanoke. They may also have helped

This strictly hypothetical view of the settlement of Roanoke Island was used as an illustration in Katherine Byerley Thomson's *Life of Sir Walter Raleigh* (Philadelphia: J. and J. L. Gihon, 1850), p. 32.

him establish his authority over the Indians around Pamlico Sound and possibly as far as the Pamlico River, over which Wingina had earlier exercised some degree of authority. It seems unlikely that the former Indian inhabitants of Roanoke Island, last heard of in Dasemunquepeuc on the mainland opposite, accepted Manteo's authority. They may well have moved out of the area. What his relations were with the Weapemeoc group of villages on Albemarle Sound or with the strong Chowan tribe on the river of that name we cannot even guess.

Can it be assumed that the Englishmen settled fairly comfortably on the island and that they survived the winter without any serious loss? This is not established, but the solidity of the palisade they built suggests that it is likely. They would expect White any time after Easter; they would, perhaps, wait with increasing impatience from May onward, but there is no assurance that they would stay after June 1588, because of a new and surprising development.

We have only two pieces of evidence concerning the whole regions of the Outer Banks and the Chesapeake between 1587 and 1590. The first case is that of a landing that Capt. William Irish made, probably shortly after White left Roanoke in August 1587. It is not known whether the location was on the Outer Banks or on Chesapeake Bay. A privateer, the *Swallowe*, under Captain Irish had been part of a squadron sent out by Sir George Carey, governor of the Isle of Wight and a probable backer of White's expedition. On its way home the ship put into "St. Mary's Bay" for water and fuel and also to see how the Roanoke settlers were faring. Irish reported that he found there a stray mule and some traces of cattle but no people. A Spanish sailor that Irish captured and who later escaped was examined at Havana, but his deposition is too vague to be of much value. Irish indeed appears to have tried to make contact with the colony. But even if he had, we could not tell at which place, since to the Spanish the name "St. Mary's Bay" (Bahia de Santa Maria) could have meant either Pamlico Sound or Chesapeake Bay. It is thus impossible to tell whether or not this evidence constitutes anything of value. The mule and the cattle seem more likely to have been on the Outer Banks or Roanoke Island than on Chesapeake Bay. If, however, they were on Chesapeake Bay, Irish was closer to the colonists than any white man was to be again. Perhaps he gave up too quickly.

The other piece of information is more specific. The Spanish at St. Augustine had for several years been planning an expedition to find the English settlement that they knew had been established farther north. Only in 1588 did Vicente González succeed in piloting a *barco luengo*, a pinnacelike vessel, into Chesapeake Bay. He made a thorough exploration of the bay, the first on record, but found no trace of an English settlement and saw few Indians. On his way back he kept close to the shore from Cape Henry southward and eventually found an entry into the sounds. He located Roanoke Island and at an unknown date in June sailed into Roanoke Sound. He reported that "on the island shore, on the inside of the little bay they had entered, there were signs of a slipway [the Spanish *varadero* used here often means a shipyard, but this would hardly be applicable in this case] for small vessels, and on land a number of wells made with English casks, and other debris indicating that a considerable number of people had been there." The entry was probably Hatarask, used by the colonists, and the little bay a now-eroded inlet well to the north of modern Baum Point; another breach in the Outer Banks somewhat to the north (the Port Lane of the 1585 colony?) is also mentioned. González saw no one and did not pause to search. No report of what he said on this subject to the then governor at St. Augustine, Pedro Menéndez Marqués, has thus far been found, but the latter certainly planned an expedition to wipe out the colony, if he could find it, before he was recalled to Spain and his expedition indefinitely postponed.

This episode is interesting because it suggests that the cove used by the colonial visitors since 1585, at no great distance from the fort, revealed signs of relatively recent use, probably in the form of broken containers and artifacts. This could well have been debris left from the embarking of the main body of colonists for several trips by the pinnace up Currituck Sound to the vicinity of their new home. But it is interesting too that there was no sign of the pinnace there. This would suggest that the approach of the Spanish vessel had been observed well in advance and the pinnace hidden around the north end of the island in Albemarle Sound. Or it might mean that at this time the colonists left behind were not on the island awaiting White but were at Croatoan with Manteo. If they were on the island, they kept well hidden. And if they had not already built their defensive palisade, they may have done so following the appearance of the Spanish vessel, so that they would not be caught without defenses at a later time. On the whole, the assumption that the men left behind on Roanoke Island did not spend much time there after the Spanish vessel discovered the location of the original colony may be justifiable. If they did leave, they were very wise. If Spain had acted quickly, the English might easily have been caught and perhaps even made to reveal where the main colony had settled.

Whenever the small group left as a body to live at Croatoan—though they could visit Roanoke Island from time to time in a day's sail—they could not take with them the heavy gear that the main body of colonists had left behind: the brass and iron guns (seen by John Lawson over a century later), the bars of iron, and the chests of personal property with which Gov. John White had entrusted them. The metal was simply left where it lay—White's chests with his armor, pictures, maps, and instruments being carefully placed in the bottom of a trench that was reopened where it had originally been dug under the orders of Philip Amadas in 1585 (perhaps part of the ditch of the old fort perimeter restored as Fort Raleigh in the twentieth century). Foraging Indians eventually found these items and may well have removed some clothing and light metal objects. They were not interested in paintings or maps, though it is strange that they did not take the armor to cut up for knives and weapons. This material is likely to have been buried in 1589 rather than in 1588 because the paper survived, even though the armor had rusted, until the late summer of 1590, when White finally appeared. Or it might possibly have been put away earlier, since the desertion of the island may have taken place soon after the Spanish appearance.

The men left their marks for White to follow if he did come (and they still had some idea that he would)—the letters "C R O" carved on a tree on the way from a landing place near the old fort site and, more decisively, on the bole of one of the debarked trees that formed part of the entrance to their compound, the word "CROATOAN." There is little reason to doubt that, having done this, they would have remained with Manteo near modern Buxton over the winters of 1588–1589 and 1589–1590. By this time, separated from their friends for so long, it would have been easy for them to identify with the Indians. If anything like the original number (which we have arbitrarily put at some twenty-five) survived, they would have been sexually deprived and attracted by any unmarried Indian girls they met (though Harriot said the original colonists had not been). Manteo, having spent the better part of the two years in England, would have been unlikely to put tribal restrictions in their way, though he probably would have insisted on firm unions between individual men and women and not permitted a promiscuity that could disrupt the social patterns of the tribe. The Englishmen would have been taught fishing and hunting, as well as the slash-and-burn technique of clearing ground for gardens, which the women would plant. An accession of male strength of this order would have been very welcome to a tribal unit that may not have been very numerous, provided that in the wider and more fertile Outer Banks of the time there was enough arable land to support the newcomers. And indications from recent archaeological research are that coastal peoples of the area derived more of their sustenance from the almost inexhaustible marine fauna—oysters, crabs, and fish—than from corn and crop growing generally.

It might be expected that, by the summer of 1590, the men of 1588 had become at least partly incorporated into a native American society, if still new and strange to it in many respects. Did Manteo's formal admission to the Church of England in 1587 mean that the Englishmen would reinforce the Christianizing of their adopted society? This is only one of many questions that no attempt can be made to answer, but it may be worth considering. Since there was no later contact with the colonists, no one can tell. Whether the pinnace was ever used again and whether an attempt was made to reach the main colony by sea is not known. The answer is, probably not, as the pinnace may not even have survived until August 1590. The story of these three years contains a few facts—the building of a protective structure, the visit of the Spanish expedition, and the indications of the men's destination after leaving the island—and many assumptions, which appear not unlikely to have some validity.

V. John White Returns in 1590

In 1590 John White was a passenger on board the man-of-war *Hopewell*, diverted against the will of her crew to cruise along the North American coast instead of sailing back to England with her consorts to make sure that captured goods, and even a captured Spanish ship, arrived safely home and, more importantly, that her own crew's share of the prize money was kept for them. She was not inclined, therefore, to waste time on John White's call. The *Moonlight* was more at his command, and her captain had probably been instructed to convey White and the occupants of Roanoke Island, assuming they were found there, to Chesapeake Bay. But misfortune overtook this ship. Capt. Edward Spicer of the *Moonlight*, who was in the leading boat of two that sailed through Hatarask Inlet on August 17, was drowned with six of his men when the boat overturned in rough water. This was a considerable blow to White, perhaps a fatal one, as it was to prove.

Capt. Abraham Cocke of the *Hopewell* was a strong, experienced voyager, and he salvaged the overturned boat and had White rowed in another vessel to the island in the early hours of the eighteenth. Previously, guns had been fired to attract attention, and natural smoke from burning vegetation was taken as evidence of occupation on the Outer Banks. The men anchored in the channel that is now Roanoke Sound and sounded trumpets, sang songs, and called as they made their way up the eastern channel. They landed near the northwest point of the island, seeing tracks of Indian feet in the sand (White must have recognized the broad, unharnessed footmarks as Indian), and then went onshore. They saw the tree with "C R O" marked on it and then reached the place where the 1585 houses had been. They found the new compound standing intact in that place and, by the entrance, the debarked tree with "CROATOAN" on it with no accompanying sign of distress. It had been recognized in 1587, with some prophetic forethought, that members of the colony might not still be on the island when White returned. It was therefore agreed that they should inscribe clearly where they had gone and should add an indication, in the form of a cross (which a printer later made a Maltese cross) above the inscription, if they were in danger. There was no such sign, so that White could imagine with almost complete certainty that the residual party was at Croatoan with Manteo and his people. (We might wonder, however, what sign they could have made if they had been suddenly attacked and overpowered by a large, hostile group of Indians!)

White proceeded to uncover the remains of his own possessions, his pictures and maps spoiled by rain and his armor rusted because scavenging Indians had dug the storage chests from the ditch in which they were buried and then had left them. These tangible signs of loss, even more than the absence of the people he hoped would meet him, were hard for him to bear. But relief was in sight: let him, with sufficient seamen to take him by water, go across Pamlico Sound to Manteo's village and all would be well. No one seems to have even suggested walking fifty to sixty miles down from Hatarask Inlet to Chacandepeco, the inlet at modern Cape Hatteras, and then making contact across it, as they would have been very near the village. The obvious course of action was to go across Pamlico Sound by water, but with the loss of Spicer and his men in mind and with water still rough, perhaps in the wake of a hurricane, such a proceeding involved considerable risk. Too, White's authority (and he had never shown himself capable of standing up to seamen when they opposed him) was greatly weakened by Spicer's death. Abraham Cocke's men on the *Hopewell* were tough fighters of Spanish soldiers and sailors and had no interest whatever in the Lost Colonists. They were desperately anxious to get to sea again. It is true that Cocke did express the intention of going back to winter in the Caribbean, but, even if he meant it, it is unlikely that he could have made the crew obey him. In any case, White makes it clear in his narrative that they did not try to get the boats into the sound, since the sea had become so rough that anchor cables were no longer adequate to hold the ships in the roads.

The *Hopewell* was driven southward and dragged and eventually lost some anchors, so that only one of four cables and a single anchor were left. It was now essential for the vessel to leave North American shores and return to England. The *Moonlight*, with her inadequate remaining crew, sailed on ahead. The *Hopewell* did get sight of the *Moonlight* again near the Azores. Other privateers, well known to them, were also in the vicinity of the islands, as were some of the queen's ships which were waiting, unavailingly, to capture Spanish treasure vessels. Without joining them, the *Hopewell* steered for home, and on October 24 White landed at Plymouth.

This mid-nineteenth-century sketch depicts a ship such as might have been used by the Lost Colonists. From Benson J. Lossing, *The Pictorial Field-Book of the Revolution* (New York: Harper and Brothers, 2 volumes, 1860), II, 243.

Whatever White expected, Sir Walter Ralegh had literally no time for him. Ralegh was in Ireland attending to his great new plantation in Munster. It is probable that White went to seek him there and was induced to give up his search, at least for the time being. Ralegh was too much involved in Ireland and in other matters to launch another Virginia voyage. White had ascertained, if indirectly, that some members of the 1587 colony were still alive or could reasonably be assumed so. Ralegh's own right to a monopoly on English enterprise on North American shores would end in April 1591, if he had not by that time established a colony. So long as the presumption that the 1587 colony, or some part of it, still existed in America was maintained, his monopoly held good. He could pick up the Virginia enterprise again, therefore, as it suited him to do so and could uphold his right against any others in the meantime, although so long as war lasted he would have few competitors. Indeed, at that very time Spain was having to give up elaborate plans for settling her own colony on Chesapeake Bay and deny it forever to the English.

VI. The Long Desertion of the Colonists

Ralegh had established himself in Ireland in the old coastal town of Youghal in 1589, had become its mayor, and was successfully developing English settlements on his vast estates in east County Cork and west County Waterford. He had induced Thomas Harriot to come to his aid by getting him a lease of extensive abbey lands and buildings at Molana Abbey on the River Blackwater. It is almost certain that Ralegh induced White to stay in Ireland by reviving the old partnership between him and Harriot, having them draw out topographical maps of his new holdings (42,000 acres plus wasteland) on both macroscopic and microscopic scales. At one time it was thought that White's holding was well to the west in County Cork (near where the poet Edmund Spenser was settled), but it now appears to have been on the eastern border at Ballynoe (Newtown) in the barony of Kilmore, at no distance from Harriot's estate at Molana. Harriot's visits to Ireland were few and far between. Nothing is known of when they occurred except that at the time of his death he held documents on Ralegh's rents in Munster in his possession, and so it may be assumed that he went to collect them from time to time. However, there are several maps and plans known that can possibly be attributed to him or to him and White jointly. It might seem that White settled in Ireland, perhaps bringing a wife from London or finding one there. But he did not forget his colonists. Richard Hakluyt had printed narratives of the 1584–1588 voyages in his *Principal navigations* in 1589, and he wanted an account of the 1590 voyage from White. It was sent on February 4, 1593 (or possibly 1594), with a covering letter from "Newtowne in Kylmore."

White stressed to Hakluyt that the instruction given to the *Hopewell* and the *Moonlight* in 1590 had not been observed, and that the vessels had brought him too late to Roanoke Island and had given him inadequate help there. This is probably true, but the occurrence of sudden storms, often lasting some days, was not confined to August and later months; White could have encountered similar conditions in June, though this was less likely. In his letter White wrote as one who had finally given up all hope of seeing his daughter and her family again. He wished to God the voyage had been as prosperous to him as it might have been and not so "discomfortable" to the colonists. But he would endeavor to remain contented with his lot and give up attempting to return to America, since his means were not "answerable" to his will. He could see no prospect of having another expedition equipped to search for the settlers. He could only commit them to God's mercies and leave it at that. The sadness and fatalism of this letter have remained his testament from its publication in the new *Principal navigations* in 1600 to this day. For White the colony was lost indeed.

VII. The Chesapeake Settlement: Conjectures

All contact with the Lost Colonists proper, the main body of whom can be assumed with some confidence to have settled in what is now Norfolk County, Virginia, is lacking from 1587 to at least 1603. At the end of this time Virginia Dare, if she survived, would have been more than fifteen years old and so of marriageable age by both English and Indian standards. This gives us some measure of what time would have done to the settlers. Those who had been in their twenties when they left England were in, or approaching, their forties; those who had been forty were, by the standards of the time, old men and women of fifty-five or more. If they lived healthy lives—and the chances are that, barring a conflict with Indian neighbors, they did—the eighteen females might be presumed to have given birth to at least two children each and to have reared, at a conservative estimate, one each. If deaths among the original men, women, and children were not more than eighteen, a little more than one a year, then the community of eighty to 100 persons would have remained about the same size it was at the first settlement. Under very favorable conditions the group could have been larger; under less favorable conditions, smaller. This observation merely puts the possible scale of survivors into some perspective. However, if there were about seventy males (including the boys who would have reached the age of puberty) and only eighteen females, then more than fifty of the men would have had to cohabit with Indian women or remain without partners. It might reasonably be expected that at least half of them found Indian women with whom they could live and bear racially mixed children. On this basis it is estimated that the number of English and part-English could have reached 150 or even gone somewhat higher.

The colonists would have, it is thought, erected a village based at first on thatched pole-and-frame houses, with wattle-and-daub filling used as they became established. They could conceivably have made brick for hearths and even chimneys. Too, they might have erected a palisade of stout poles joined by riven planks such as archaeologist Ivor Nöel Hume has found at Martin's Hundred in Virginia. As the English settled more firmly, they would be not unlikely to build a communal structure to use as a church and for community activities, as was done in Jamestown at a very early stage. There would have been wells and outhouses and enclosures for breeding rabbits and perhaps other livestock (they may even have had some fowls with them), and horses and mules in small numbers may have accompanied them, though this is very doubtful since they apparently failed to acquire livestock in the Caribbean (though we should not forget Captain Irish's mule). They had at least one mortar with them and some handguns, judging by what John Smith later learned. The settlers would also have needed a storehouse, or more than one, for harvest products. There would have been garden plots, possibly small fields like those used by the Indians and probably mainly for Indian crops, though some English seeds could have survived the winter of 1587–1588.

The small segment of an Indian village that has recently been excavated on the west side of Broad Bay, linked with Lynnhaven Bay and near Virginia Beach, is likely to have been a Chesapeake community of some size. It is farther west than White's Chesepiuc but

This representation of the first attempt by the English to settle North America was used as an illustration in S. G. Goodrich's *Pictorial History of America* (Hartford, Conn.: E. Strong, 1846), p. 330. It, like virtually all such representations, is purely hypothetical.

could possibly be the same village. What remained at the site when professional excavation became possible in 1981–1982, according to E. Randolph Turner of the Virginia Research Center for Archaeology, was "part of a palisaded village with two longhouse structures inside it . . . , the first in coastal Virginia to be clearly identified archaeologically." This is very valuable information. Another site is also known which could be the Apasus added in the engraved version of White's map. But Skicóac was a long way to the west of these sites, some fifteen to twenty miles from modern Virginia Beach. The Chesapeake settlements, however, appear to have been very similar to those of the Indians of the North Carolina sounds that White's drawings depict.

With our very limited knowledge of the Chesapeakes we cannot estimate how large the tribal group may have been. If Skicóac was in fact a very large village and if there were more than two other villages (the one on Broad Bay may have been an additional settlement), it might be guessed that, having remained independent of Powhatan for a long time, the Chesapeakes numbered at least 1,000 people. If assimilation occurred, the settlers would have adopted Indian ways of living to a considerable extent, perhaps transforming their village into an Indian-style one or even amalgamating with Skicóac or another community. With the opportunities for hunting, fishing, and agriculture that the area afforded, such a village, no doubt separately organized at first, could enjoy a good living, given the absence of war, internal dissension, and epidemic disease, none of which can be eliminated. But since the only evidence there is indicates that the colonists lived peaceably, losses by war can probably be ruled out. We are told that they intermingled with the Indians, which would certainly mean there were interracial alliances that would have produced children neither wholly English nor wholly Indian. Everything else that has been said is conjecture; but it can be assumed that there was a considerable degree of cultural assimilation, with the interpenetration of customs and techniques and with, more than possibly, a Christian tinge overall— even if there was no direct conversion of the Indian tribe to Protestant Christianity—since the colonists are unlikely to have surrendered wholly their faith and religious practices.

After twenty years, however, their Englishness would be wearing thin; they would be approaching virtual assimilation. If this happened, it may be incorrect to think of them as completely English or as vitally concerned with renewing contact with their countrymen. No certainty about this exists; but if intermixture went as far as has been suggested, the colonists were in almost every way very unlike the people who set out from Roanoke Island in 1587, and their children were perhaps totally different. Whether or not a site on which they lived will ever be found we cannot tell; but if so, it would contain at least some European artifacts, even though Powhatan looted the settlement in addition to killing the colonists. There would be at the very least some pottery fragments and possibly other things, lost or thrown away or remaining after the killings and the almost certain clearing of the site. Substantial remains should be found if the settlement is ever located.

Until 1603 the Lost Colonists remained alive in English legal fiction. Sir Walter Ralegh proposed going to look for them in 1595 but never did so. His experiences on his Guiana expedition obliged him to return home without calling at Croatoan or Chesapeake Bay to see whether any Englishmen were still alive. Then about 1599 he began sending small expeditions to collect medicinal roots—sassafras and china root and gums thought to have medicinal properties—along the shores near where the colonists might be. It was natural that he focused his search on Croatoan, since that was a precise location to which some were known in 1590 to have gone. Even if White believed the main body had moved fifty miles away to Chesapeake Bay, he could not tell exactly where they were located; therefore, Ralegh's men stood less chance of finding them there, especially as White knew that their village might be located well inland from Chesapeake Bay. Only detailed information from men left on Roanoke Island would be of any real assistance. Before 1603 none of Ralegh's ships made any contacts that gave clear indications of the whereabouts of any white person living along the shores of what is modern North Carolina, but there may have been hints, if coastal Indians were encountered, of such persons living well to the north of the Carolina Outer Banks. As early as 1592 there had been a rumor, circulated no doubt to divert the attention of Spanish agents and reported by them, that Richard Hawkins, who was preparing to set sail in that year, was bound for Virginia and not for the South Sea. This story was, of course, false, but it represented a continuing Spanish belief that there was an English colony living there. In 1600–1602 this idea was still maintained in Spanish Florida, and in 1603 and again in 1606 the constable of Spain gave it as his opinion that the English had for a long time been occupying the coast.

John Gerard, the herbalist, took for granted in 1597 that in "Virginia . . . are dwelling at this present Englishmen," unless disease had wiped them out. A law court took a different view and in 1594 applied the rule that seven years' loss of contact implied death of the person concerned, so that the estate of White's son-in-law Ananias Dare, which included some property in London, was administered in that year on the assumption that Dare was deceased. In 1600 the Reverend George Abbot expressed in print the probability that all contact had been lost and the country left to its original inhabitants, but Richard Hakluyt, his fellow clergyman, was more cautious in the third volume of *Principal navigations*, the second edition of which he published in 1600. He printed White's 1593 (or 1594) letter that implied that the settlers were still alive and in another passage noted that some plans were afoot to revive colonization, although he did not commit himself in any way to the idea that the earlier colony had survived up to the time of publication. It is clear that the one reconnaissance we know a little about, that of Samuel Mace in 1602, did not get farther north than modern Cape Hatteras, if that far. If Mace encountered any Indians, and it is not known that he did, he might have picked up some hint, which he did not follow up, that there were white settlers living far to the north. Ralegh's actions in 1603 might indicate that Mace did bring home some suggestion that Chesapeake Bay should again be explored.

VIII. The Colonists Believed Alive, 1603–1605

The years 1603 to 1605 present more substantial, but still circumstantial, indications. It seems very likely, though it remains to be proved by precise evidence, that news at second hand reached England of the survival of the settlement in the vicinity of Chesapeake Bay and that this was publicized in ways about which nothing certain is now known. It is known that in 1603 Ralegh engaged Bartholomew Gilbert and Samuel Mace to go to Chesapeake Bay with two ships to look for the colony, having presumably reviewed his former efforts and considered them misdirected. The voyage of Bartholomew Gilbert in the *Elizabeth* of London (fifty tons) was a disastrous one; he repeatedly failed to find the entrance to Chesapeake Bay, went ashore somewhere either north or south of the entrance to Delaware Bay, and was killed, as were several of his men, by an Indian war party on which they stumbled. The master of the ship, Henry Sute, brought the ship home with a crew of only eleven men and boys, reaching the Thames toward the end of September.

About Mace's voyage there is no direct information whatsoever, so what follows must remain circumstantial; but indications seem to point in a single direction. A distinct possibility is that Mace made his way into the bay and sailed up the York River, there encountering a number of Indians belonging to Powhatan's tribe, several of whom he induced to come on board and then kidnapped them. It is certain that men were taken by someone, since Powhatan complained in 1607 that "two or three years before" (but it could well have been four years) some of his men were seized and carried away. Indians had been brought to England from the Roanoke Island area in both 1584 and 1586, so that language and local conditions could be learned from them before a colonizing expedition was sent out. If Mace's ship brought these men from Chesapeake Bay, it must have arrived in London at the very end of August 1603. On September 2 or 3 a Thames wherry towed an Indian canoe and carried some Indians up the Thames to the landing place leading to Lord Cecil's house in the Strand. In subsequent days they gave displays of handling the canoe for Sir Walter Cope, an enthusiast for American colonization, and others, in the absence of Sir Walter Ralegh (accused of treason and a prisoner since July in the Tower of

London) and of Lord Cecil (Robert Cecil, better known by his later title of earl of Salisbury), who was attending the king in Hampshire because the court had moved out of plague-stricken London. Ralegh's monopoly of American colonization had reverted to the king, and there was no one to take responsibility for the Indians except Cope, who may have continued to do so if they were not killed in the plague. If they were brought by Mace, and if they had come from the York River, Thomas Harriot, at least, could have spoken to them in their own language and learned whether white settlers were still living in association with the Chesapeake Indians in the south of the bay. He could even have taken them to Syon House, where he was in the earl of Northumberland's service. But Harriot was lying low, since his long association with Ralegh made him suspect. He had, however, given some help in preparing Mace's expedition in 1602. Though the suggestions made here are far from certain, word apparently circulated that settlers still survived in North America.

Twice in 1604 George Waymouth, a member of a seagoing and shipbuilding family, presented to King James I versions of a treatise called "The Jewell of Artes," which suggested various projects for helping navigators and voyagers. Among them he included no fewer than six rather fanciful plans for towns, as well as for a number of castles, to be built by and for colonists in America. He urged the erection of fortified towns and castles "in the land of Florida [which term could cover the whole east coast of North America] in those parts thereof which long have been in possession of our English nation . . . as but weakly planted with the English and they more weakly defended from the invasions of the heathen, amongst whom they are . . . subject to manifold perils and dangers. Whereas it being so fruitful a soil, so abounding with woods [and] so goodly rivers . . . those parts might easily be fortified and well planted with the English." He thus took for granted that the Lost Colonists were no longer unlocated but that they survived and ought to be reinforced and strengthened. Indeed, it would appear that he assumed King James was already familiar with information that something had been heard of the Lost Colonists or his observations would not have been easily intelligible to the king. King James, it might be concluded, was being reminded that he had subjects living in Virginia for whom he was now directly responsible.

It is also likely, though no direct evidence has yet appeared to establish it, that a ballad or broadsheet was circulating in London with some exaggerated material about the Lost Colonists in it. The play

Eastward Hoe, an entertaining romp in which three distinguished playwrights—George Chapman, Ben Jonson, and John Marston—had a hand, was produced in London in 1605. It contained a well-known jibe about settlers in America making their fortune: "A whole Country of English is there man, bred of those that were left there in 79 [*sic*]. They have married with the Indians and make them bring forth as many beautiful faces as any we have in England, and therefore the Indians are so in love with them that all the treasure they have they lay at their feet." This reference could make no sense to a London theater audience eighteen years after the colony had been left behind in America if there had not been some popular publication to which it alluded or if the Ralegh colony story was not well known. A ballad or broadsheet might have stressed the survival of the colony by inter-marriage with the Indians and the supposed golden tribute resulting from the mingling.

This network of references seems to make feasible the conclusion that something, whatever precisely it was, about the survival of the Lost Colony reached London between 1603 and 1605. It may be worth noting too that Capt. Christopher Newport, who was to be chosen in the following year to command the English expedition to the Chesapeake that founded Jamestown, had an audience with King James after a Caribbean voyage in 1605 at which he presented the king with an alligator or crocodile. It is conceivable that Newport collected the creature on the southeastern shores of North America, and if so he may also have reconnoitered the route to Chesapeake Bay that he was to pioneer in 1606. It is worth remembering that, on bringing the "second supply" to Jamestown in 1608, he was specially instructed to search for the Lost Colonists.

One of the most unexpected pieces of evidence that the Lost Colonists were believed to be alive and still to be found at Croatoan in 1604 comes from the interrogation of prisoners at St. Augustine who were captured by a Spanish force in St. Helena Sound with the ship *Castor and Pollux* and her consort. This expedition sailed under a French license but in English ships with an English captain, John Jerome of Plymouth, who may well have known about the Roanoke voyages from persons who had taken part in them. This Anglo-French venture was to trade in the Caribbean. It was to make its way through the Caribbean and then sail along the coast of North America from Florida to the Bay of Fundy, trading where possible. Unfortunately, it got only as far as the site occupied by the Cusabo Indians of modern South Carolina, at St. Helena Sound, before it was overwhelmed by a Spanish naval squadron in March 1605.

Instructions for this voyage compiled in England in May 1604 had directed the ships to call at Croatoan, where there were Englishmen settled, and to trade with them for the herb "Oyssan" or "Bissanque." The cape merchant of the expedition (in command after Captain Jerome had been killed), a Frenchman named Bertrand Rocque, when asked about Croatoan, in which the Spanish naturally had a great interest, answered that "he does not know where the said place is, but he understands that its latitude is thirty-six and a half degrees, and they were to go in search of it along the coast, and that he does not know how many Englishmen are settled there, but he believes that they came to settle fifteen years ago, and he does not know with what authority except that they were sent by an Englishman called 'Guater Rale' [Walter Ralegh], who himself brought them and left them the first time [showing that the myth of Ralegh's personal establishment of the first colony was already current] and now they had to go in search for them." Rocque was then asked what the herb "Oyssan" or "Bissanque" was: "he says that he has not seen it, but he knows that when the Englishman 'Guatarrale' came to settle some Englishmen, they took some of the said grass to England and announced that the Indians spun it to make cloth, and they worked it in England and saw that it was silk, like that from China, and for that reason he was to seek it along this coast and take back what he could, and he believes that it is to be found where the English are settled." There is some confusion here between yucca fibers and the expectation that the seedpods of the *wisakon* or milkweed were suitable for silk making. Samples of cloth from the yucca were mentioned in Thomas Harriot's *Briefe and true report* in 1588. John Gerard had mentioned and illustrated the milkweed (but as a medicinal plant) in his *Herball* in 1597.

The capture of the *Castor and Pollux* and her smaller consort was the reason that the Spanish sent Ferdinand de Écija to search for the colony later in 1605, but he did not get even as far as Cape Fear before returning without news of any English settlement. The Anglo-French expedition of 1604–1605 showed, however, that some people in England believed there was still a viable trading colony living with Manteo's tribe at Croatoan and that the expedition could exchange with it for milk-weed and other products some of the many utensils, tools, and weapons they carried. Unfortunately the ships were frustrated, and it will never be known what, if anything, they would have found on Croatoan had they reached it. But clearly, not all hopes of the survival of at least some of the Lost Colonists were centered on Chesapeake Bay.

IX. The Colony and the Chesapeake Tribe Destroyed

It is now necessary to deal with the crucial question of the personality, authority, and actions of Powhatan. For several decades before 1606 he had been building up his authority in the Virginia tidewater, subjugating by diplomacy or war, or both, tribes along the James and York rivers and on the Virginia Eastern Shore. Not all the tribes on the south bank of Chesapeake Bay and the James River were prepared to acknowledge his authority, at least on a permanent basis. And at least one tribe on the north bank of the James, the Chickahominy, retained substantial autonomy, perhaps because of their military skill. Among the tribes that evidently did not pay tribute to Powhatan was the Chesapeake. Moreover, if our reading of events is correct, these Indians were harboring and making marriage alliances with a group of white refugees who had appeared many years before but apparently had not played any part in the politics or warfare of the area and so had not been molested. But the entry of a Spanish ship into the bay in 1588 must have given Powhatan some grounds for concern, though this vessel did not make any effective contacts with the white refugees or with any of his own dependent tribes. After 1588, however, no European ship is known to have entered the bay until 1603 at the earliest. If an English ship sailed there in 1603 (under Samuel Mace) and took away several of Powhatan's men by force, the incident would have aroused his fears of European intervention. It is likely that Powhatan kept a continuous lookout for further intruders. In addition, he is not unlikely to have put pressure on the Chesapeake Indians to submit to his authority and perhaps to have demanded that they hand over the assimilated white persons to him, assuming the earlier discussion of their status is correct.

William Strachey's later statement that the Lost Colonists, and apparently the Chesapeakes as well, since they were intermixed, were slaughtered "at what time" Christopher Newport's ships entered the bay will be discussed in detail below. If this statement is taken literally, the massacre would have taken place very quickly between April 24 and 27, 1607, and the evidence of it would have been covered up, at least to some extent. This assumption places Powhatan in a position to take punitive action on a large scale at a moment's notice and is not easily reconcilable with our general understanding of Indian resources, but it is not impossible. Otherwise, the massacre must have occurred shortly before this time and on the strength of prophecies by Powhatan's priests that white men would soon come to deprive him of his kingdom, as the English were to assert was the immediate cause of his action. If the lookouts posted on Cape Henry from about April 24 onward were Powhatan's, then the killings probably took place appreciably earlier than the actual sighting of Newport's ships *Susan Constant, Godspeed,* and *Discovery.*

There is, however, a complex story to unravel concerning what happened after the three ships sighted the entrance to Chesapeake Bay and made their way into its mouth. It is by no means certain that our evidence is sufficient to set the record straight, but from that point onward there is specific information to rely on. Once around Cape Henry, Captain Newport's party landed a little to the west of the cape on April 26 and found their first sight of the country favorable. At night their camp was attacked by a party of Indians coming from "the mountain" (which can only be an uneroded Cape Henry), who wounded several of the English and were dispersed by gunfire in the direction from which they came. These Indians were later believed to be members of the Chesapeake tribe, but it is very doubtful that they could have been.

"Provisioning, 1589" is the title of this engraving. Still another flight of fancy, it appeared in an article entitled "Loungings in the Footprints of the Pioneers," published in *Harper's New Monthly Magazine.* XVIII (May 1859), 761.

The explorers then moved to Lynnhaven Bay, where they assembled their knocked-down pinnace and on the twenty-seventh explored the bay, seeing in the distance only a small party of Indians, who retreated to "the mountain." They followed a stream entering Lynnhaven Bay on April 28 and "saw a plain plot of ground," George Percy, who recorded these events, said, "where we went on land and found the place five miles in compass without either bush or tree." This may have been due to local geological conditions, but the land might more plausibly have been cleared recently and used for settlement. There was no Indian settlement to be seen, though in White's day there had been at least two Indian villages in the vicinity. It might be suggested by implication that all evidence of occupation had been cleared from the area by Powhatan's force.

The exploring party proceeded some miles farther, apparently to the west, where all they saw before reaching the forest was a "great smoke of fire" that they believed had been set by the Indians (Powhatan Indians?) to a large expanse of grass. This too might be construed as a cover-up of indications of Indian or Indian-white settlement. On proceeding through the burnt-off area, Percy reported that they passed "through excellent ground full of flowers . . . and as goodly trees as I have seen." He went on to say: "Going a little farther we came to a little plot of ground full of fine and beautiful strawberries," but in "all this march we could neither see savage nor town." Though the explorers went back to their pinnace and moved over to the north shore without reaching the Elizabeth River on the south bank, it is very difficult to believe that the Chesapeake Indians, even if not the surviving Lost Colonists, could have been in any part of the area that the party explored without showing signs of their existence and of their dwellings and fields. Still, we cannot exclude the possibility that the surface geology of part of the area favored meadows rather than arboreal cover. But the assumption that the hostile bowmen that Newport's explorers first encountered were Powhatan's men makes it appear highly probable that the principal inhabitants had been killed or removed. At the same time, there is every indication that Powhatan and his subordinates determined to keep alive the idea that the attackers were Chesapeake Indians and that the English would do well to stay clear of them.

If this interpretation is correct, what occurred when Newport's party reached the falls of the James River below modern Richmond, after Jamestown had been chosen as the settlement site and a party had gone ahead to explore the river to the west, was an elaborate charade.

Rarahunt, one of Powhatan's sons (Tanx Powhatan), pretended to be the great chief himself and solemnly declared that all tribes of the region acknowledged him as their overlord except the "Chesepians" alone, whom, Gabriel Archer reported, "we perceived to be an enemy generally to all these kingdoms." Since it was the Chesapeakes who were said to have attacked the settlers at their first landing, Archer reported, "I took occasion to signify our displeasure with them also, making it known that we refused to plant in their country." This was precisely what Powhatan wished, so that his destruction of the tribe and his killing of the colonists would remain unknown to the English.

The area was not left uninhabited, however. William Strachey later reported that "such new inhabitants that now inhabit 'Chessapeak' again (the old extinguished as you have heard . . .) are now at peace with him [Powhatan]." Capt. John Smith, from what he heard, estimated the strength of the Chesapeakes, as he thought them, at some 100 fighting men. But not until he published his *Generall historie* in 1624 did he give any account of his penetration into this area at the end of his final expedition up Chesapeake Bay, when he entered what was apparently the Elizabeth River at the beginning of September 1608. He wrote that "because we had only but heard of the 'Chisapeacks' and the 'Nandsamunds,' we thought it as fit to know all our neighbours near home, as so many nations abroad. So setting sail for the southern shore, we sailed up a narrow river up the country of 'Chisapeack.' It hath a good channel, but many shoals about the entrance. By that we had sailed six or seven miles. We saw two or three little garden plots with their houses, the shores overgrown with the greatest fir trees we ever saw in the country. But not seeing nor hearing any people, and the river very narrow, we returned to the great river." There Smith soon encountered the Nansamond Indians, who submitted only after a fight. The "new inhabitants" of whom Strachey was to speak several years later kept wholly out of sight, presumably because it would become clear, if they were encountered, that they were not the original Chesapeakes at all. Subsequently, until well after 1622, we have no record of any Englishman setting foot on this territory, so that its secrets never came to light.

So far as the story of how the massacre of the Lost Colonists became known can be reconstructed, it begins with the unguarded statements of Powhatan to Capt. John Smith at his last meeting with the Indian ruler in December 1608. Smith made no mention of this conversation in any of his published writings, probably because it might have reflected unfavorably on him. If the Virginia Company, proprietors of the Jamestown colony, suspected that he had withheld from them information that was apparently sent confidentially to King James in order to obtain his reaction, this might have worked to Smith's disadvantage. The king's response to Smith's disclosures took the form of instructions that were issued in May 1609, by the Royal Council for Virginia, not the Virginia Company itself, to deal with Powhatan for his crime. In 1623 Samuel Purchas would write in his tract "Virginia's Verger," published two years later, that "Powhatan confessed to Captain Smith that he had been at their slaughter and had divers utensils to show." Moreover, Purchas added a note to his large compilation *Pilgrimes* in 1625 saying that "Powhatan confessed that he had been at the murder of that colony and showed to Captain Smith a musket barrel and a bronze mortar and certain pieces of iron which had been theirs." There is no doubt that Purchas got this information from Smith himself, who was cooperating closely in collecting material for *Pilgrimes* for some time before it appeared, and that it was true. Smith's suppression of his knowledge of the massacre for so long is a principal reason that its occurrence has been treated skeptically by later historians.

The other main authority for information concerning the killings is William Strachey, appointed secretary to the Jamestown colony in 1609 but shipwrecked on Bermuda and thus prevented from taking up his post until 1610. He remained in Virginia for over a year, putting its records in order and compiling his own account of what had happened since 1607. He reported "how that his Majesty hath been acquainted that the men, women and children of the first plantation at Roanoak were by practice and commandment of Powhatan (he himself persuaded thereunto by his priests) miserably slaughtered without any offence given him." It may be suggested that the confidential letter, no longer extant, by John Smith to King James informing him of the massacre was dispatched toward the end of 1608 and reached England in the spring of 1609. The Royal Council for Virginia, at the king's command, gave instructions in May 1609 to Sir Thomas Gates, who was going to Virginia as lieutenant governor when his ship, *Sea Venture*, grounded on Bermuda.

The instructions contained two significant passages, the second of which reads: "For Powhatan and his *weroances* it is clear even to reason beside our experience that he loved not our neighborhood, and therefore you may in no way trust him, but if you find it not best to make him your prisoner, yet you must make him your tributary and all other his *weroances* first to acknowledge no other lord but King James and so we shall free them all from the tyranny of Powhatan." The first passage expresses the view of the council that "we think it reasonable you first remove from them their *iniocasockes* or priests by a surprise of them all and detaining them prisoners. . . . And in case of necessity or convenience, we pronounce it not cruelty nor breach of charity to deal more sharply with them and proceed even to death with these murderers of souls and sacrificers of God's images to the Devil." A later passage relates the priests directly to the massacre. These instructions would have been in Strachey's charge while his party was stranded in Bermuda and would have been brought by him to Jamestown at the time Sir Thomas Gates eventually arrived there as lieutenant governor with his colonists (in improvised vessels) in 1610. It should be noted, too, that the instructions were reissued to Lord De La Warr when he went out as governor in 1611. Strachey, in his "Historie of Travell into Virginia Britania," completed in 1612 but written mainly in Jamestown during 1610–1611, makes clearer what was implied by these instructions. The massacre was reported to King James, Strachey said, and "because his Majesty is of all the world the most just and mercifull prince, he hath given order that Powhatan himself, with his *weroances*, shall be spared and revenge only taken upon his *quiyoughquisocks* [priests, spelled otherwise above], by whose advice and persuasions was exercised that bloody cruelty, and only now that Powhatan, himself, and the *weroances*, must depend on his Majesty, both acknowledging him for their superior lord." He goes on to explain that the detaching of the subordinate tribal leaders (*weroances*) from Powhatan and their direct attachment to and dependence on the English would be acceptable to these leaders, as the arrangement would offer them great advantages and relieve them of many burdensome exactions. This, it is obvious, would have involved splitting up the Powhatan Confederacy into its constituent parts, an action that the English never felt strong enough to attempt while Powhatan was alive.

It is clear that the killing of the Lost Colonists was known in England early in 1609 and that formal arrangements for what Strachey considered a very limited measure of punishment for Powhatan and his dependents were made in that year. Yet because of the failure of the instructions to arrive on time and the desperate condition of the colony in 1610 and its continuing weakness even into 1612, these plans were never executed. There is no doubt, however, that Powhatan was held responsible for the violent and bloody end of the Lost Colony.

It is Strachey who provides the most information on when the Lost Colonists were killed, saying that for "twenty and odd years [they] had peaceably lived and intermixed with those savages [the Chesapeakes] and were off his [Powhatan's] territory." Considering that Strachey might not have known precisely to the month when the Lost Colonists arrived in the Chesapeakes' territory, this would date their massacre as late as 1607. His statement that they lived peacefully with the Indians and intermingled with them is the source of earlier suggestions on this subject. Elsewhere, Strachey spoke of "the slaughter at 'Roanoke' at what time this our colony (under the conduct of Captain Newport) landed within the 'Chesapeack Bay,' " which would place the killings toward the end of April 1607, a possibility already considered, assuming that "at 'Roanoak' " and, elsewhere, "of 'Roanoak' " mean not Roanoke Island but the settlers of the Roanoke colony that had moved to the Chesapeake area.

The killing of the Chesapeakes is dealt with by Strachey in a separate section of his "Historie" concerned with Indian wars. Prophecies by the priests lay, he wrote, behind many of Powhatan's violent actions. He continued: "Not long since it was that his priests told him how that from the 'Chesapeack' Bay a nation should arise which should dissolve and give end to his empire, for which not many years since (perplexed with this devilish oracle), according to the ancient and gentile custom, he destroyed and put to sword all such as might lie under any doubtful construction of the said prophecy, as all the inhabitants, the *weroance* and his subjects of the province, and so remain all the 'Chessiopeians' at this day, and for this cause, extinct."

It has already been indicated that if the Lost Colonists were living among the Chesapeakes and were indeed intermingled with them, the massacres of the Lost Colonists and of the Indian tribe must necessarily have taken place at the same time. It has also been indicated that while they may have occurred toward the end of April 1607, they could, indeed, have happened a little earlier. If so, we might wonder (with no evidence to support the idea) whether the priests could actually prophesy the impeding arrival of the English colony or whether they were farsighted politicians who had argued, from the appearance of a foreign vessel in the bay a few years earlier, that the proper time to strike potential enemies close by—namely the Chesapeakes and the Lost Colonists—was before any such intruders reappeared. In the latter case, coincidence led to the killings taking place in 1607, though whether or not at the precise time that Newport's ships appeared on the horizon it may never be possible to tell.

X. The Search for Survivors

Once the Virginia Company came into existence in April 1607 and began preparing to settle both north and south Virginia, the latter being Chesapeake Bay and the area to the north and south of it, locating the Lost Colonists clearly became a high priority. Not only would it be a matter of national pride to establish contact with English people who had been lost for twenty years, but also the settled colonists could be of great value to the new colonists in providing them with information on the nature and condition—not to mention the languages—of Indian society. They would have accumulated a mass of invaluable knowledge on how to establish a community successfully, grow crops, prospect for minerals, and perform innumerable other tasks. There is not in the "Instructions by way of advice" of 1606 any requirement that the Jamestown colonists find the Lost Colonists, but we lack specific details of what they were to do, apart from these rather general prescriptions for settling, and it is almost certain that finding the colonists ranked among their practical aims. It may well be that Newport had enough hints from information that had come to England about the location of the colonists to induce him to make some discreet inquiries concerning their continuing survival, but we do not know how far he did so.

One problem confronting us is that we do not know how much of the language of the Powhatan territory the English could speak or understand. Thomas Harriot had helped Samuel Mace in 1602 by providing him with some sort of vocabulary, and it is now known that he had devised a system for pronouncing Algonquian as he had heard it in the colony of 1585–1586 and had compiled some sort of dictionary of the language. His phonetic system has survived, but the vocabulary, or dictionary, appears to have been destroyed in the Great Fire of London in 1666. Harriot knew the Virginia colonist George Percy, a brother of the earl of Northumberland, who had been living at Syon House where Harriot resided and may have taught him a little of the language since Percy, in the narrative he wrote about the first contacts of the colonists in 1607, suggests he was not wholly ignorant of what was being said by the Indians and may even have been able to speak a little. Gabriel Archer had been in contact with Indians who spoke several of the New England dialects in 1602 and may have been sufficiently interested in language to have taken lessons from Harriot before setting sail for Virginia. It is Archer who provides the first coherent accounts of conversations with Indians encountered in the early stages of exploration of the James River; and it may be presumed that he did not invent what he reports, though he may have exaggerated his understanding in order to give his report continuity and meaning. Christopher Newport certainly was anxious to pick up Algonquian words as he traveled up the river, but this does not necessarily mean that he studied the language before he set sail or had picked up more than a few words, perhaps, from Percy and Archer on the voyage. However, the historian must consider the question of language in order to judge what these early observers learned, or heard, about the Chesapeake Indians and, perhaps, about the Lost Colonists, though contemporary accounts say nothing directly about the latter.

Capt. John Smith, an experienced traveler, had certainly developed a technique for acquiring a small working vocabulary from new peoples with whom he came in contact, but he had things to do other than attempt an interrogation of the local Indians to see if they could tell him anything about the Lost Colonists. It was not until the end of 1607, when Smith was captured by Opechancanough and brought to Powhatan's chief town of Weromocomico on the York River, that he had any chance to try to use such vocabulary as he had acquired to make inquiries about the Lost Colonists. He did so, and the Indians told him that some members of their community had been seized a few years before by a white man; they thought at first that Smith was that man. Having examined him, however, they found that he was not; yet they told him nothing about the fate of the Lost Colonists at their hands. Instead, Opechancanough and Powhatan separately, concealing all knowledge of the Lost Colonists as such, told Smith a vague story that there were clothed (white) men still living well to the south, at a place called Ocanahonan. This could have been a mere tale, even though it was supported by later investigations. The Indians also told Smith about another group far to the north (this group being, genuinely enough, the French).

In his published writings of 1608, 1612, and 1624, Smith said nothing about hearing news of the Lost Colonists during his long expeditions around Chesapeake Bay and up its rivers during 1607–1608. He did, however (probably following instructions brought by Newport in January 1608), make some effort to search for them to the south of the

James River. He enlisted the services of Wowinchopunk, chief of the Paspahegh Indians. This man had hitherto been hostile but at this time wished to win Smith's approval and agreed to go with two of the settlers to search well to the south for the village of Ocanahonan, which may have existed on the Chowan River, on the Roanoke, or even farther south. Smith wrote that the chief cheated him and returned in a few days, but it is now clear that he did not and that he and the two Englishmen continued much farther south. It is evident from inscriptions on the so-called Zúñiga map, now in Spain and with which Smith was involved, that the explorers entered the Roanoke River region and heard reports of copper deposits at a place called Ritanoe (conceivably in the Virgilina ridge, where natural copper was found in the nineteenth century). They explored farther inland or to the south (or both) and heard that, at a village called Pakerikanick, "remain the four men clothed that came from 'Roonock' to 'Okanahowan.'" This apparently meant they were persons who had escaped from the Chesapeake massacre and not men who had been with Manteo. They were reported to remain there still, but the searchers did not succeed in reaching them.

A report on this expedition, which has not survived, was the basis for further entries in the orders given by the Royal Council for Virginia in May 1609. These instructions, also discussed earlier, told Sir Thomas Gates to establish an additional settlement farther south, in modern North Carolina, where "two of the best rivers [the Roanoke and the Chowan] will supply you. Besides you are near to rich copper mines at Ritanoe and may pass there by one branch of this river, and by another Peccarecomicke." This latter name may be the Pakerikanick already mentioned, but London officials could not be expected, in the absence of adequate maps, to understand the topography of the Carolina sounds. However, they added the statement that at the latter place "you will find four of the English alive, left by Sir Walter 'Rawley,' which escaped from the slaughter of Powhatan of Roanoke upon the first arrival of our colony." The four men were therefore identified, correctly or not, as survivors of the massacre of 1607. Gates was told that "they live under the protection of a *weroance* called Gepanocon, by whose consent you will never recover them. One of these were worth much labor." This chief may have been the ruling head of the Chowanoac tribe, and the reason there was no optimism that he would release them was, apparently, that they were employed in working copper for him. Thus some coherent story reached England about the survival of a few of the members of the Chesapeake colony, though whether or not it was accurate it is impossible to say.

The Virginia Company took note of the 1608 report only in 1610 when its official pamphlet, A *true and sincere declaration . . . of the plantation begun in Virginia* (London, 1610), reported that "intelligence by some of our nation planted by Sir Walter Ralegh, yet alive, within fifty miles of our fort . . . can open the womb and bowels of this country, as is testified by two of our colony sent out to seek them, who, though denied by the savages speech with them, found crosses and letters, the characters and assured testimonies of Christians cut in the barks of trees," reminiscent of the signs left for White in 1590. But that was all. Contact was not maintained, and the survivors were never found.

A further strand of the story was derived by William Strachey from a friendly Indian, Machumps, who in 1610 or 1611 built on this report and told Strachey that at "Peccarecanicke" and "Ochanahoen" the people had houses built with stone walls and one story above another, "so taught them by those English who escaped the slaughter at 'Roanoak' at what time our colony . . . landed within the 'Chesapeack' Bay." The tale that houses built of stone were inspired by English survivors sounds unlikely, though the teaching of construction of two-story houses made of poles and timbers is not incredible. The Indian went on to say, or so Strachey reports, that "at Ritanoe the *weroance* 'Eyanoco' [the Gepanocon discussed above?] preserved seven of the English alive, four men, two boys and one young maid, and fled up the river of 'Choanoke' [Chowan], to beat his copper, of which he hath certain mines at the said Ritanoe." The latter part of this statement is specific enough. It would seem to imply, however, that the Chowanoac tribe, with which Lane had close relations in 1586, had by 1608 temporarily pushed back the Mangoaks [Tuscarora] of Lane's time from at least part of the Roanoke River basin and had acquired natural copper deposits there. This is considered highly improbable by authorities on the Tuscarora. The acquisition of substantial amounts of copper by trade seems more probable, and the possession of a mine by the Chowanoac tribe most unlikely. The retention of refugees from the Lost Colony massacre who may well have adapted themselves to living with another Indian tribe is intelligible in these terms, if the white people knew how to harden copper by hammering and annealing so that it could be used for tools and weapons. Additional information is thus far lacking.

The first search made for the Lost Colonists has been followed, so far as possible, into 1609, but it was not the only search made in 1608. Newport came to Virginia in October 1608; and among his orders was one to bring back "one of the lost company sent out by Sir Walter Raleigh," though Smith mentions this in a sneering way and does not indicate that Newport made any attempt to seek for survivors. But Smith himself did something. In December 1608 he sent out two parties. One, under Michael Sicklemore, penetrated as far as the Chowan River and returned with some news about the country into which the colonists of 1585–1586 had traveled "but found little hope and less certainty of them [that] were left by Sir Walter Ralegh"—a report that could well have been elaborated. In the other search, Nathaniel Powell and Anas Todkill were conducted by another Indian tribe living south of the James River into the territory of the "Mangoages," the Iroquoian Tuscarora who were the copper-owning Mangoaks that Lane looked for up the Roanoke River in 1586. The search was thus temporarily diverted to the interior in the southwest. The expedition was without result. Smith said after its return that "nothing could we learn but they were all dead" but once again failed to give the reasons for his conclusion. Later, Smith gave some description of the country the searchers passed through and mentioned that the language of the Indians there differed from that in Virginia, pointing to the fact that these Indians belonged to the Iroquoian language group and making clear their identity with the Tuscarora. For North Carolinians the knowledge that a considerable portion of the eastern part of their state was explored as a result of the search is of interest, as is the proposal, which was not implemented, for creating a settlement on the Roanoke River.

At some time after Newport had left the colony and before the end of 1608, Smith learned from Powhatan of his part in the massacre of the Lost Colonists. One possible reason for his silence on this subject in published works has already been suggested, though he did charge Powhatan with other killings. Another possible reason for not pub-lishing the confession was that in 1608 Powhatan had been given insignia sent to confirm him as a dependent of King James and it would have been unwise for Smith to declare publicly that he must now be treated as an open enemy without having King James's permission. It is even possible that Smith had learned that the ceremony in 1607— when he believed he was being prepared for execution and was saved only by the intervention of the young Indian Pocohontas—really meant that he was being received into Powhatan's circle as a *weroance* and so had become, formally at least, a vassal of the murderous ruler who later brazenly admitted the slaughter of the Lost Colonists. Smith was a proud man and a social climber; and he would not wish his part in the earlier dealings with Powhatan to become known, though he could report confidentially to King James what he had learned in December 1608 of Powhatan's direct responsibility for the killings. It was only in conversation with Samuel Purchas some fourteen years after his return from Virginia that Smith admitted that he had specific admissions from Powhatan that he had killed the Lost Colonists.

It is strange that even though it was known by 1609 and confirmed in 1610 or 1611 that survivors of the Lost Colony were apparently living at no great distance from the James River and were employed in copper working by the man assumed to be the chief of the Chowanoac tribe, no concerted attempt was made to recover them. Whether or not a military operation was possible is unclear—the colony remained in a tenuous state for some time, and an adventure of this sort might have been thought too risky. But it was not out of the question to send emissaries to the Chowanoac chieftain with bribes that he could scarcely refuse. However, the potential value of survivors to the colonists decreased as the colonists became familiar with the country and needed less help from them. After 1611 it may have seemed to most Jamestown settlers mere sentimentality to expend any great effort to recover a few individuals. Under the spartan regime of Sir Thomas Dale, 1612–1616, this seems plausible. But evidence is entirely lacking. The survivors were deserted completely, so far as is known, for twelve or thirteen years, and all chance of making the earlier much-desired contact was lost. Nothing is known from these years of attempts to search the Outer Banks for colonists who had remained with Manteo. They are never even mentioned and pass into oblivion for the rest of the seventeenth century.

XI. The Last Search— and an Epilogue

When John Pory went to Virginia as secretary to the colony in 1619, it may have been love of exploration or even a touch of sentiment (he had helped Hakluyt compile the second edition of *Principal navigations* and had been steeped in the story of the Lost Colony) that led him to renew the search. He was the first person, in all this long period, known to have made his way southward from the James River to the area where survivors of the massacre of 1607 were supposed to have taken refuge. George Sandys wrote from Jamestown on March 3, 1622, about his expedition as far as the Chowan River and gave some description of the country as characterized by great forests and excellent corn-growing soil. The Indians there tried to tempt him to visit a copper-producing area—the one already mentioned or perhaps another. Pory's own narrative has been lost, but John Smith reported his lack of success in finding out anything about the Lost Colonists. All that remains is Smith's epilogue stating that, after thirty-five years, "we left seeking our Colony, that was never any of them found, nor seen to this day in 1622." The handful of fugitives had been allowed to vanish; the last little group of which there is any tenuous knowledge slips finally into oblivion. In any event, if even one of them was alive in 1622, he or she would have been so thoroughly Indian in outlook and culture that the past in a white community near the Chesapeake Bay, let alone in England before 1587, would long have faded or died.

There were Indians on Roanoke Island when Francis Yardley finally went there in quest of land in 1653, and they were friendly and willing to cooperate with the Englishmen. They had nothing to say about how the earlier colonists had met an end except to point out the evidence of the "old fort," the remains of the perimeter of the 1585–1586 fort and not the enclosure of 1587–1590. In 1701 John Lawson visited not only the fort site but also Croatoan Island, by then known as Hatteras Island. The Indians there may have been descendants of Manteo's band, as Lawson described them as differing from the other Indians of the area, though many changes of population could have taken place in the meantime. Lawson wrote:

These tell us that several of their ancestors were white people and could talk in a book [that is, read] as we do, the truth of which is confirmed by gray eyes being found frequently amongst these Indians and no others. They value themselves extremely for their affinity to the English, and are ready to do them all friendly offices. It is probable that this settlement miscarried for want of timely supplies from England or through the treachery of the natives, for we may reasonably suppose that the English were forced to cohabit with them for relief and conversation and that in process of time they conformed themselves to the manners of their Indian relations.

The handful of Hatteras Indians of 1701 can be seen, if we wish, as the mixed descendants of those who, expecting White but not waiting long enough for his arrival, had gone to Croatoan and more than a century later revealed themselves by their features, traditions, and mixed ancestry. (In fact, the Moseley map of 1733 recorded six or eight Indians as still living at Hatteras.) But the time span is too long for certainty. Other groups may have been shipwrecked on the Hatteras shoals and found refuge with and been assimilated by the native society, or refugees from the Virginia colony could have reached there; but if we wish to have a myth of continuity from the Lost Colonists to the white settlement of modern North Carolina, it can be found here. It may be myth, but it is not wholly without historical foundation, even though it is far from being fully established.

Looking back, it can be said that the Lost Colonists, in both their group near the Chesapeake Bay and, probably, that near modern Cape Hatteras, have strong claims to being the first enduring English communities on the North American continent. No more is known about their way of life, or even where they died, than was known in the seventeenth century, but accounts by their contemporaries do give substance to the belief that the settlers represent not simply sojourns by a few parties of transient English people in the sixteenth century. Instead, they provide a strong element of continuity with the seventeenth century shared by the modern states of North Carolina and Virginia, who thus conceived and maintained the first English settlements, whose quadricentennial was fitly commemorated in the 1980s.

XII. The Value of the Sources

For 1587 and 1590 there is no question of the truth and accuracy of the material that John White has left on record. The historian's regret is that White did not say more about the establishment of the colonists in 1587 and give more precise details of where they intended to go when they left Roanoke Island. John Smith, writing between 1608 and 1624, is more difficult to judge. The account of him given in these pages shows him to have been devious and selective in telling, or not telling, what he knew. He was also, as readers of his works will know, inclined to magnify his own part in events. Yet in factual matters he has been found accurate and reliable, where his map can be compared with his narrative and both can be compared with other contemporary sources. At the same time, for sixteen years Smith hid the information that he had explored up the Elizabeth River in 1608, and only in private did he reveal, between 1623 and 1625, that well before he left Virginia in 1609 he knew of the destruction of the Lost Colony by Powhatan. But Smith's statements on these points can be accepted at face value as true. They are too circumstantial not to be so.

William Strachey, as secretary of the Virginia Company's colony from 1609 to 1611, was thoroughly reliable and conscientious in what he wrote. Between 1610 and 1611 he collected at Jamestown all the information he could about the early history of the colony from the best sources he could find (including, it is believed, a draft of Smith's *Map of Virginia* that was published in 1612), though he was not in Virginia from 1607 to 1610 and had to get his facts about these first three years from other persons and sources and consequently could not verify everything he wrote. Strachey's most important statements about the Lost Colony are confirmed by an official document, the instructions of May 1609, and it is almost certain that what he says on the subject can be relied upon or at least that his statements were based on the best information he could obtain. Some of the skepticism shown by North Carolina historians about Smith and Strachey has resulted from inadequate knowledge of their work and, especially, of how far they could be relied upon. Modern research has established their basic authenticity.

Suggested Reading

The story of the Lost Colony in its context can be read briefly in David B. Quinn, *Ralegh and the British Empire* (New York: Macmillan Co., Collier Books, revised edition, 1962; Harmondsworth, Middlesex: Penguin Books, revised edition, 1973) and in David Durant, *Ralegh's Lost Colony* (New York: Atheneum, 1981). The details on the Lost Colony, to which it has been possible to add just a little since publication, are given in David B. Quinn, *England and the Discovery of America, 1481–1620* (New York: Alfred A. Knopf, 1974), 432–481.

The documentary material that gives us our evidence on these events will be found in Richard Hakluyt, *The principall navigations, voiages and discoveries of the English nation* (1589) a facsimile edited by D. B. Quinn and R. A. Skelton (Cambridge, Eng.: Hakluyt Society, 2 volumes, 1965); *The principal navigations, voyages traffiques & discoveries of the English nation*, III (London: G. Bishop, R. Newberie and R. Barker, 3 volumes, 1598–1600) and VIII (Glasgow: J. MacLehose, reprint edition, 12 volumes, 1903–1905); and John Smith's *Works* (Birmingham: Edward Arber, 1884; Edinburgh: J. Grant, 1910). Modern editions are David B. Quinn, ed., *The Roanoke Voyages* (Cambridge, Eng.: Hakluyt Society, 2 volumes, 1955); D. B. Quinn and A. M. Quinn, eds., *Virginia Voyages from Hakluyt* (Oxford: Oxford University Press, 1973) and *The First Colonists* (Raleigh: Division of Archives and History, Department of Cultural Resources, 1982); P. L. Barbour, ed., *The Jamestown Voyages under the First Charter* (Cambridge, Eng.: Hakluyt Society, 2 volumes, 1969); William Strachey, *The Historie of Travell into Virginia Britania*, edited by L. B. Wright and V. Freund (London: Hakluyt Society, 1953); and D. B. Quinn, A. M. Quinn, and S. Hillier, eds., *New American World: A Documentary History of North America to 1612*, III and V (New York: Arno Press, 5 volumes, 1979). These provide all the evidence we have.

Specialized aspects are dealt with in William S. Powell's "Roanoke Colonists and Explorers: An Attempt at Identification," *North Carolina Historical Review*, XXXIV (April 1957), 202–226, his *Paradise Preserved* (Chapel Hill: University of North Carolina Press, 1965), and his *John Pory* (Chapel Hill: University of North Carolina Press, 1977); Jean Carl Harrington, *Search for the Cittie of Ralegh* (Washington: National Park Service, 1962); and D. B. Quinn, "An Anglo-French 'Voyage of Discovery' to North America in 1604–5, and its Sequel," *Miscellanea offerts á Charles Verlinden* (Ghent: Ghent University Press, 1975), 513–534.

Index

T

Tanx Powhatan, 40
Thames, 5, 33
Tobacco, 1, 16
Todkill, Anas, 48
Towaye (Native American), 8, 9
Tower of London, 33-34
Trade/Trading, 1, 17, 35
True and sincere declaration . . . of the plantation begun in Virginia, A (pamphlet), 47
Turner, E. Randolph, 30
Tuscarora, 47, 48

V

Vessels, 12, 19, 20, 26, 42. *See also* Boats; Canoes; Pinnaces; Privateers; Ships *and by individual name*
Villages, 1, 8, 17, 18, 28, 30, 39. *See also by individual name*
Virginia: colony in, 51; Eastern Shore of, 37; Indians of, xviii, 3, 48; map of, 52; N.C. as England's first, 1; Ralegh's enterprises in, 25; settlers in, xvii, 28, 44
Virginia Beach (present-day), 29, 30
Virginia Company, x, 41, 44, 47, 52
Virginia Eastern Shore, 4, 37
Virginia Research Center for Archaeology, 30
"Virginia's Verger," (tract), 41
Voyages, x, xvii, 7, 14, 25, 33, 36

W

Wanchese (Native American), 4
War/warfare, 1, 2, 30, 37
Warr, Lord De La, 42
Warren, Lindsay C., xi

Waterford, County, 26
Waymouth, George, 34
Weapemeoc, 18
Weapons, 2, 12, 20-21, 24, 36
Weather conditions, 4, 5, 10, 13, 24, 26
Welsh, 5
Weroances (tribal leaders), 41, 46, 47, 48
Weromocomico (Indian town), 45
White, Elenor. *See* Elenor Dare
White, John (governor): abandons attempts to return to colony, 13, 14, 25, 27; believed colony moved inland, 31; descriptions of Roanoke by, 10, 16, 17; in Ireland, 26; letter by, 32; map by, 17, 29, 30; narrative of, 24; reports on colonial settlement, 8, 10, 11, 52; returned to England for supplies, 12, 13, 15; Roanoke Island colony led by, ix-x, xvii, 4, 6; voyage of, in 1587, 6-7. *See also* Colonists, Lost; Roanoke Island
White-Harriot map, 16
Wingina (chieftain), 8, 18
Wisakon (milkweed), 36
Women, 2, 6, 21
Wowinchopunk (chief), 46
Wright John, 8, 9, 15

Y

Yardley, Francis, 50
Yeomen, 5
York River, 16, 33, 34, 37, 45
Youghal, 26

Z

Zúñiga map, 46